W9-DDI-263

I Am
A Woman
By God's
Design

Beverly LaHaye

I Am A Woman By God's Design

Fleming H. Revell Company
Old Tappan, New Jersey

Unless otherwise identified, Scripture quotations in this volume are from the New American Standard Bible, Copyright © THE LOCKMAN FOUNDATION 1960, 1962, 1963, 1968, 1971, 1973, 1975 and are used by permission.
Scripture quotations identified KJV are from the King James Version of the Bible.
Excerpts from *Humanist Manifestos I and II,* edited by Paul Kurtz, published by Prometheus Books, 1203 Kensington Ave., Buffalo, N.Y. 14215, used by permission.

Library of Congress Cataloging in Publication Data

LaHaye, Beverly.
    I am a woman by God's design.
    Includes bibliographical references.
    1. Woman (Christian theology) I. Title.
BT704.L34   261.8'344   80–24461
ISBN 0–8007–1131–9

This book is lovingly dedicated to two very important people in my life: to my darling, aged mother, who presented me with the opportunity to live and gave me an early start in being the girl God fashioned me to be; and to my faithful, loving husband, who has encouraged me to develop and experience the fulfilling role of womanhood and to reach the full bloom of God's design for me. My prayer is that this beautiful privilege of being a Christian woman, with all the benefits of godly femininity, will not be denied my daughters and granddaughters and all the daughters to come.

Contents

Introduction

This subject is too controversial to handle without using an authority that is unchanging and consistent. The topic of women's roles and rights in today's society can vary as much as changing fads and women's styles. In fact, year after year, it takes on a different emphasis, which can be as shifting as the seasons.

It is true that over the centuries women have been victims of cruel custom, tyrannical tradition, and inferior status, but that is not the honor that Scripture has given to women.

Therefore, it becomes important that the foundation of such a discussion be an absolute—one that comes from an authority above any human wisdom. The greatest and only authority would be the Creator of all living things, who could best explain why He created male and female and the specific purposes of each. "For in Him all things were created, both in the heavens and on earth, visible and invisible, whether thrones or dominions or rulers or authorities—all things have been created through Him and for Him" (Colossians 1:16).

God also inspired chosen men to write that Scripture: "All Scripture is inspired by God and profitable for teaching, for reproof, for correction, for training in righteousness; that the man of God may be adequate, equipped for every good work" (2 Timothy 3:16, 17). In other words, the Scripture has been verbally inspired by God. He breathed out His divine teaching, to be written down for the benefit of those who would seek to know the truth.

It is this solid and unchanging authority that has been used as the foundation for this book. When the subject of the creation of male and female is considered and the wife's role in relation to her husband is discussed here, the discussion is not based on the changing wisdom of man, but on the unalterable truth of the Word of God.

The greatest controversy arises from those who use Scripture only when it benefits their argument. When Scripture disagrees with them, they explain it away as tradition that is not current with the times. This philosophy has been used by the women's-rights movement, since it allows them to keep one foot in Scripture and one foot in the liberal element of a new movement. But the Word of God is absolute and unchanging. It has stood through the ravages of time and will be the final authority to judge us by, when we stand before our Maker: "Forever, O Lord, Thy word is settled [stands firm] in heaven" (Psalms 119:89).

My strong motivation in writing this book is threefold: 1. to encourage those godly women who believe they are designed by God and accept His role for them; 2. to reach out to other women who believe God to be the Creator of all things but have become confused by the voices of the women's movement and are caught in the tug-of-war between humanism and God's law; and 3. to offer a strong defense against those who deny the existence of God and declare women will only be free when they throw off the shackles of religious belief that bind them.

It is my great concern that this truth be shared with the many women of the world who are seeking to be liberated—seeking, but never quite finding, the freedom for which they look. Their quest for freedom will go on unendingly, unless they heed the truth from the very God who created them: "If you abide in My word, then you are truly disciples of Mine; and you shall know the truth, and the truth shall make you free" (John 8:31, 32).

A clearer understanding of woman's spiritual relationship to God, and living in that relationship, are the only bases for total freedom and liberation.

I Am
A Woman
By God's
Design

1
Woman-Chance or Design?

If I had been allowed to choose, would I have chosen to be a woman? First of all, I know it was not possible to choose. Secondly, at the time our sex was determined, who of us had enough wisdom about the pros and cons to make a wise choice? But, putting all that aside, if the choice were yours to make, would you choose the sex you are? If your answer is yes, then you have taken the first step toward self-acceptance. It is important to like yourself as God created you. If you are not certain that you agree with the sex that has been assigned to you, then other complications may follow, as a result of this uncertainty.

By Mistake or Choice?

How was our sex determined? Was it by chance, or someone's choice? Could a mistake have been made? All of these questions and more have definite answers, when we accept the biblical teaching on Creation. Confusion begins when we deny God as the Creator and attempt to place our origins in the hands of chance. Many questions go unanswered when we talk about evolving, without wisdom and design, from a lesser creature. It is easier for me to accept myself and fully approve of who and what I am, when I acknowledge that I am the result of a master design—one with definite plans and purpose for my being. I love being a woman! Not because it suits my emotions, which it does; not because it matches my physical characteristics, which it does; but because I am assured that this was God's choice and design for me. God, who created all things and designed the master plan for the universe, is a Creator with order and purpose. Therefore, I know that, as a woman by God's design, I also have a definite purpose to follow and fulfill. When a woman does not like her sex, she lives in conflict with her purpose and potential for life. Women need to recognize and accept the truth that God did not create them inferior.

Built According to Blueprint

In the first two chapters of Genesis, we read the story of Creation. As we follow each step, it is interesting to note that God puts His stamp of approval on each finished product.

The first day, God created light and separated light and darkness, "And God saw that the light was good . . ." (Genesis 1:4).

On the second day, God made the heavens and the dry earth and gathered the waters to be called seas, "and God saw that it was good" (Genesis 1:10).

It was the third day that God brought forth vegetation and plants yielding seeds to bear after their kind,

"and God saw that it was good" (Genesis 1:12).
The fourth day was when God made the sun and moon to govern day and night, and then He added His touch of beauty by sprinkling the stars in the heavens, "and God saw that it was good" (Genesis 1:18). On the fifth day, God filled the sea and the air with living creatures, "and God saw that it was good" (Genesis 1:21).

It was the sixth day when God populated the earth with the beasts and everything that creeps on the ground, "and God saw that it was good" (Genesis 1:25). However, He was not finished yet. God then created man in His own image, male and female. "And God saw all that He had made, and behold, it was very good . . ." (Genesis 1:31).

The only negative note in Creation was, "Then the Lord God said, 'It is not good for the man to be alone; I will make him a helper suitable for him'" (Genesis 2:18).

Understand that this newly created man was not totally alone. After all, God had spent the previous days creating every living creature in the sea, in the air, and on the dry ground. God even lined up every one of His new creatures and asked this new man to give them a name. There were birds and beasts of every description, but God knew that man could not live with only the companionship of creatures. The Creator could have created another man for fellowship or given him an animal for a partner, but neither would have been a "helper suitable for him." Man needed a helper who would be suitable and give him completion. This was to be a special creation. Man was formed of the dust of the ground. Then God took a rib from the man and fashioned it into a woman. She came into existence from something already created; in other words, she was an extension, or a part of, man (Genesis 2:21, 22).

I find an interesting comparison here, which reveals my female sex. Genesis 1:27 says that God "created" man, but Genesis 2:22 tells us that God "fashioned" the woman. This word comes from the Hebrew root word meaning "to build" or "to design." God had a special blueprint and design for woman, so He fashioned her into what He wanted her to be. Could it possibly be that God took extra care in making woman, so she could be a fairer sex and a feminine beauty? She was designed to complement the man, not to replace him.

God's Course for Correspondence

The account in Genesis is no accident or mistake! It was God's premeditated plan. The woman was designed to correspond to the man in all areas: physically, emotionally, mentally, and spiritually. "For man does not originate from woman, but woman from man; for indeed man was not created for the woman's sake, but woman for the man's sake" (1 Corinthians 11:8, 9).

Unless a woman believes the Bible's teaching of

creation by God, she cannot readily accept this concept that woman was created for man.

A Ship off Course

Those who deny Creation and the existence of God—atheistic humanists—are also some of the leaders of the women's-rights movement who are denouncing the roles of women and would, if they could, change the course of purpose and direction for every woman hereafter. The fundamental teaching of the religion of humanism is that the universe is self-existing, not created, and that man is a part of nature that emerged as a result of a continuous process.[1]

No wonder the followers of humanism are demanding vast changes in women and our society. They do not believe that woman originated from man and was created for the man's sake. They do not understand the plan of the God who made us, who controls life and death, and who will judge us one day for our deeds on this earth. The woman who is not motivated and guided by God's plan for her is like a ship without a course, a locomotive without an engineer.

The problems increase when a woman will not accept that she was created from and for man, with a specific purpose to fulfill. She begins to question who she is. Why is she here? Why should she be different from a man? Why can't she exchange roles with a man? Why should she be a "baby machine"? Why does she have to care for the children? She begins to believe that this God-created difference is really discrimination toward the female sex.

A woman who does believe that God was the Creator of all things has little problem with accepting who she is and what her divine purpose is in life. She will find her fullest joy when she fits in with the design and instruction of her Creator.

Limitation or Liberation?

The sex God has assigned to each is important, but even greater than the male and female identity is our association with the One who made us. It is a necessity to identify with Jesus Christ, in close fellowship with our Lord and Saviour. Then the sex differences seem to fall into proper perspective and order.

The fashioning of woman was no mistake. The greatest mistake of all is when a woman will not accept her divinely appointed role and purpose for living. Then she becomes bound up in her own limitations and cannot experience the true liberation that comes from accepting the truth—and the truth shall set her free.

2
Fashioned by God

There are many uniquenesses of women. One of the more materialistic is that women have always been interested in style and fashion. Down through history, you see the ladies setting the pace in changing fads and modes. Generally, women seem to be more sensitive to style than men, perhaps because ladies' designs change more frequently than do their counterparts'. Most American women have, at some time, lingered over a fashion magazine or stopped turning the pages of the newspaper long enough to brief themselves on the latest styles. Even if they never wear designer clothes, there seems to be a feminine curiosity to at least know what is available and what the rest of the fairer sex is wearing.

Designer Labels

The more elite fashion books will show models wearing clothes with a famous designer's name attached. When the society page reports a social event, there may be a description of the gowns worn by the noted ladies and a little designer name dropping.

I find it amusing that so much emphasis is put on the origin and design of clothes. A famous designer's tag does not guarantee any longer life to the garment;

nor does it necessarily mean it was made better. It does, however, guarantee a different price tag.

I well remember my disappointment in a designer dress. As a young married woman, I was given the opportunity to receive, as a gift, a dress that I could not have afforded to buy for myself. It was my first outfit with a well-known designer's tag attached. I received it with such appreciation, and I fully expected more from the dress than it was able to provide. After only three or four wearings, it began to disintegrate before my very eyes, and soon I had to set it aside, because it was beyond repair. What a letdown!

Recently, in a department store, I noticed a clever tag that may have been a result of someone else experiencing the disappointment of a famous name. This tag was made to be attached to home-sewn garments. It simply read, "My Own Creation."

Designed by the Master

Women will greatly differ on their taste in clothes, from handmade creations to designs by Pierre Cardin or Givenchy. But there is one Designer who is common to all women—from the most noted socialite to the poor, little, depressed lady in the ghetto; from the timid, soft-spoken, introverted lady to the forceful, obnoxious feminist in the news—they all have the same Master Designer! All are fashioned by God! "Know that the Lord Himself is God; it is He who has made us, and not we ourselves; We are His people and the sheep of His pasture" (Psalms 100:3).

Some will deny it; others may not care. The humanists falsely tell us, "Science affirms that the human species is an emergence from natural evolutionary forces."[1] This theory is far more difficult to accept: There is great opportunity for chance and mistake. It is more reasonable to believe in creation by God, which reveals order and purpose, particularly when we can see the evidence of God's reality revealed in human lives and nature. Only God can change the life of an individual, can transform his heart and change his direction. Only God can heal the broken heart of a parent or restore the love in a broken marriage or forgive the sins of a wayward child.

Many problems that bother women today stem from ignorance of God as the Creator and of God's love for His creation. He did not create woman to be inferior—or man to be superior. The falsely attributed traits of weakness and disorder that are attached to women can be replaced by the truth of God's love and His design for womanhood. The Bible gives sufficient warning to those who do not accept God as the Master Designer:

Woe to the one who quarrels with his Maker—An earthenware vessel among the vessels of earth! Will the clay say to the potter, "What are you doing?" Or the thing you are making say, "He has no hands"? . . . It is I who made the earth, and created man upon it. I stretched out the heavens with My hands, and I ordained all their host.

Isaiah 45:9, 12

How much easier it is to believe God is the Designer of all things, when we can see His continuing presence and existence around us.

Specially Handmade by God

Once again it comes down to the basic fact that the Bible is the inerrant Word of God. All our differences over our origin, our purpose, our role, depend on how we accept the Scripture. Is the Bible dependable and trustworthy? Do we accept it in whole or in part? In answering these questions, we need to decide whether we place a higher value on our own judgment, and reduce the authority of Scripture to mere human understanding, or yield to the conviction of John 17:17: "Thy word is truth." In deciding this important matter, we cross the line of total acceptance of the fact that Scripture is the inerrant Word of God.

Only then can I fully accept the truth in Job 10:8: "Thy hands fashioned and made me altogether" and in Psalms 119:73: "Thy hands made me and fashioned me." Accepting this truth determines how I look at myself as a woman. Because I am truly fashioned by God, I must trust Him to know what is best for me, as He determines my role and purpose in life. The unique plan for womanhood is to cooperate with God in bringing life into the world.

3
Designed to Give Life

"Now the man called his wife's name Eve, because she was the mother of all the living" (Genesis 3:20). The Bible clearly reveals God's plan for populating the earth. The union of the male and female has always been God's method for producing life. Likewise, it has been the woman's role to bear children, from the very beginning. One of the first statements that the Lord God made to Eve was, "I will greatly multiply your pain in childbirth, In pain you shall bring forth children; Yet your desire shall be for your husband, and he shall rule over you" (Genesis 3:16). This extra pain was God's judgment for her disobedience, but her role was to assist her husband in reproducing life.

In contrast, God judged Adam by cursing the ground and causing it to be more difficult to provide food for his family. The basic roles of men and women were laid out in the first three chapters of the Bible. Simply stated, the man is to be the provider, and the woman is to be the childbearer. Today there is much antagonism about this, and there are those who would try to change and upset the roles God has established. It has become possible for the woman to be the provider, but medical science has yet to help a man give birth to a child. Once again, God's absolute law and order cannot be completely reversed.

Weaving a Unique Design

The woman is God's chosen vehicle for bringing life into the world. God still does the designing, but He uses the woman's body for the growth and development of His creation. "For Thou didst form my inward parts; Thou didst weave me in my mother's womb. I will give thanks to Thee, for I am fearfully and wonderfully made; Wonderful are Thy works, and my soul knows it very well" (Psalms 139:13, 14).

When a woman has conceived, God has begun to form a human life within her. God weaves that little design in the mother's womb. Perhaps this is a contributing factor to the idea that women are basically more sensitive to spiritual teaching than men. The woman has the unique opportunity to develop a close, working relationship with God, as He creates life within her. Every time a pregnancy begins, God is performing His handiwork.

This is a living illustration of God's creative love and mercy, no matter how the pregnancy occurred. What an example of God's love and involvement with mankind. How great God is, to create a new human being, perhaps even when conceived in sin and immorality, and give him the opportunity to learn to love and to live in obedience to God's law. A man and woman may "make mistakes" or "have accidents" or "commit acts of immorality," but God is not limited by man's actions or deeds. He can bring beauty out of chaos, order out of despair, and rejoicing out of heartbreak. It is man's human reactions to these crises that will thwart and destroy God's will and power to transform situations. The act of abortion allows women to take control of areas in which God desires us to trust Him for the results.

Motherhood is the highest form of femininity. God's first instruction to the male and female was to "Be fruitful and multiply" (Genesis 1:28). Giving birth to a baby means going down into death to give life to someone else. This is a totally unselfish action. Today there is resounding ridicule of women who want to be mothers and who look upon childbearing as a high calling. The radical feminists declare that the use of the womb and the breasts to sustain life cannot be fulfilling. They say fulfillment only comes when a woman seeks out her own career, not one that has been assigned to her. But God has designed her to give life and has instructed her to be the one to conceive, carry, and nurture each little child that is placed in her womb.

Setting Historical Records

At the earliest point after conception, a human life does not look like much. The tiniest embryo is not recognizable as human, but as a living, personal identity, it is the subject of God's superintending love and concern. Scripture refers to this person as an "unformed substance" that God is skillfully designing in the depths of the mother's womb.

My frame was not hidden from Thee, When I was made in secret, And skillfully wrought in the depths of the earth. Thine eyes have seen my unformed substance; And in Thy book they were all written, The days that were ordained for me, When as yet there was not one of them.

Psalms 139:15, 16

That little unformed substance is important to Almighty God—so much so that its bones and structure are known by God. His medical history has begun! God is so interested and involved in this new creation that He records the days of his life before the natural birth has occurred: "Since his days are determined, The number of his months is with Thee, And his limits Thou has set so that he cannot pass" (Job 14:5).

Embroidered in God's Image

In the Hebrew, the words *skillfully wrought* mean intricately embroidered. In other words, a detailed pattern of design and purpose—a human life, designed in the image of God—a personal identity—has begun!

In just twelve weeks after fertilization, all the members and organs that the child will ever have are fully developed in miniature and functioning. What a miracle of life that has to be! *Figure 1* is a brief sketch of the first twelve weeks after conception: the beginning of life!

THE FIRST 12 WEEKS OF LIFE

At Fertilization	sex is determined
Week 2	occasional heart contractions
Week 3	foundations of brain and spinal cord established
Week 4	mouth is open; lung buds appear; liver is recognizable; body is ¼″ long
Week 5	rhythmic heart contractions; stomach, esophagus, intestines are defined; arms and legs appear; face looks human
Week 6	skeletal system is complete; major organ systems have formed
Week 7	traceable brain waves; responds to touch; fingers exist; cartilage is changing into bone
Week 12	brain structure complete; spontaneous movements (kicking, frowning, sucking); fully developed, functioning human body (3 inches, ½ ounce); fingerprints and individualized palm and sole lines are complete

Figure 1

God is so entwined in that little life, from conception on, that it is beyond comprehension how a woman and a doctor can choose to destroy someone so close to God's heart, created in His image. This has to be one of the most treacherous forms of child abuse! Creation and life have already been set in motion. Records of his personal identification and days of his life have been entered in God's book. How can man become a substitute god, interfering with God's divine plan for another individual?

Our value of human life will greatly influence our acceptance or rejection of abortion. How precious is a life? Dr. Bernard Nathanson, former chairman of the Medical Committee of the National Association for Repeal of Abortion Laws, states in his book *Aborting America,* "It was the cheapening of life that led to mass abortion with social consent, not the other way around."[1]

The *Humanist Manifesto II* states, "Although science can account for the causes of behavior, the possibilities of individual freedom of choice exist in human life and should be increased." But the freedom of choice that takes an innocent victim's life is never justified. The manifesto continues, "The right to birth control, abortion and divorce should be recognized." However, you cannot compare abortion and divorce, since abortion involves an unborn child who cannot speak for or defend himself. "It also includes a recognition of an individual's right to die with dignity, euthanasia, and the right to suicide. We oppose the increasing invasion of privacy, by whatever means, in both totalitarian and democratic societies."[2] This reveals little value for human life. Justice and righteousness stimulate *preserving* life, rather than yielding to an individual's "right" to *take* life. The humanist no longer recognizes a life as having intrinsic worth.

Twenty-Five-Percent Cancellations

The statistics on abortion are frightening! Unborn lives are being destroyed in America at the rate of 1 million or more a year, year in and year out. There is one "elective" abortion for every 3.2 babies born. There are those in the medical profession who argue that abortion is not the killing of the fetus, but rather the separation of the fetus from the mother. Regardless of how they define it, death of the fetus is the aim and the result of such a separation. According to Psalms 139, this substance attached to the mother's womb is a living person, for whom each and every member has been accounted.

I am again reminded that Psalms 139 says, "My frame was not hidden from Thee. . . . And in Thy book they [the days] were all written" (Psalms 139:15, 16). If the statistics given above are accurate, then one of every four babies recorded in God's book must be cancelled, because a mother has decided this baby should not live. Its days must be stricken from God's records.

If you believe the Bible to be the moral authority and God's law for mankind, then you must reject the destruction of unborn babies that is rampant in our society today.

Dr. Nathanson relates a story from the early abortion days, when a physician was speaking on his new abortion techniques:

> At the Planned Parenthood meeting in Des Moines where I first met him, Sopher (Dr. David Sopher) spoke at length on his late abortion technique. He would have a trained doctor administer general anesthesia. The cervix would have been prepared the night before by inserting a laminaria, a seaweed-based substance that would absorb fluids and swell, dilating the cervix in a matter of hours. He would break the bag of waters and quickly dismember the fetus blindly with a polyp forceps. He became so incredibly expert that his total operating time averaged three minutes, compared with the typical thirty or so minutes. He illustrated his lecture with slides in color, showing the fetus reconstructed at the end of the abortion like a grisly jigsaw puzzle. One could see where the arms and legs had been ripped from the body and removed separately, how the spine had been snapped in two and removed with dispatch, how the skull had been crushed and the brain drained out before the bony parts were removed.[3]

A contradictory scene has been duplicated many times over, in dozens of hospitals across the nation, involving two pregnant women entering the hospital for treatment. The lives within them are at similar stages of development. One woman is frantically trying to end her pregnancy by aborting her unborn child; the other is pleading with the doctor to save her child by a Caesarean section. Two different doctors go to work on their individual patients—one to destroy the life of a child, the other to use all the genius of medical science to keep it alive. If one can be saved at that early stage of development, so can two or more. When one child survives an early birth through advanced medical treatment and another dies because nothing is done in an attempt to keep it alive, that must be murder.

"Every Child Should Be Wanted"

The above heading is very idealistic and seldom realistic, plus, it demotes a child to the status of an object that can be accepted or rejected. Women have protested being viewed as objects or pieces of property, and yet these very women are inflicting this dreadful position on unborn children.

This helpless unborn must compete with other objects of "want" that occupy a family, whether it's a new sports car, European trip, stereo set, or, more practically, the refrigerator that is so desperately needed. The child has the unfair disadvantage of not being able to prove that he deserves to be accepted before the other wants. This injustice against an unborn who cannot defend himself is even greater than racial or sexual discrimination.

As Jean Garton points out:

> Yet, EVERY CHILD A WANTED CHILD fails to tell us anything about the child. If I say of you who now share my thoughts: "You are reading," "You are awake," "You are a human," I obviously would be describing you. But when I say, "You are 'wanted' or 'unwanted,' " whom am I describing? Not you! Rather, I would be telling you something about myself, for "wantedness" measures the emotions and the feelings of the "want-er." Thus the Supreme Court decision of 1973, which allows for the elimination of unborn human beings simply because they are not wanted, tells us nothing about the millions who have been destroyed legally since that date, but it does tell us what we have allowed our society to become. The unwanted child is the victim not of his own shortcomings but of those in a society attempting to solve its social, economic and personal problems by the sacrificial offering of its children.[4]

Most child abuse, whether before or after birth, is a direct result of the parents' view of life in the womb. Is the child a human life of value, or is he simply a piece of property, which can be discarded or kept? Abortion is the first act of violence (and the last) that a baby will experience from the hands of an adult.

Double Standard = Double Jeopardy

Malcolm Muggeridge, an eminent British journalist and critic who recently was converted to Christ and Christian principles, states:

Our Western way of life has come to a parting of the ways; time's takeover bid for eternity has reached the point at which irrevocable decisions have to be taken. Either we will go on with the process of shaping our own destiny without reference to any higher being than Man, and deciding ourselves how many children shall be born, when and in what varieties, which lives are worth continuing and which should be put out, from whom spare parts—kidneys, hearts, genitals, brain boxes even—shall be taken and to whom allotted, or we draw back, seeking to understand and fall in with our Creator's purpose for us rather than to pursue our own; in true humility praying, as the founder of our religion and civilization taught us: Thy will be done. This is what the abortion controversy is about, and what the euthanasia controversy will be about when, as must inevitably happen, it arises.[5]

Christians need to be more aggressive in abortion issues. If child abuse is wrong after birth, then it is absolutely wrong before birth. If destroying life is wrong after birth, then it is wrong before birth. We cannot have a double standard on justice and morality.

For Sale: Human Life—Cheap!

When the United States Supreme Court approved abortion-on-demand on January 22, 1973, it turned away from biblical standards of justice and morality, to accept those of ancient paganism. They were trying to find a right way to do a wrong deed. This was the first step toward establishing the principle that human life is cheap and can be eliminated, which has, in turn, contributed immeasurably to the increase of child abuse.

Recently a young mother in our city, thinking that she might be pregnant, decided to go to a well-advertised birth-control clinic for a free pregnancy test. After her visit, she sent me the following note:

Recently I had the opportunity to see firsthand just how little the world values human life. It is unborn life but LIFE just the same. Not having much money, I decided to go to a locally advertised birth control clinic for a free pregnancy test. While giving the counselor the necessary information about myself, she casually asked me if having another baby so soon was alright with me. If not, did I want to know what to do about it?

The walls were plastered with pro-ERA abortion-on-demand literature, casual sex endorsements (with reminder to use some kind of birth control!), and many self-help advertisements.

After seeing what the clinic stood for, I felt very

sad that I had even gone to them for help. Abortion is the only solution that the world has to offer for an "inconvenient pregnancy."

Now that I have one child, I realize that life is so precious. Because of this incident, I am taking a definite and vocal stand against abortion.

Many young women go to a birth-control clinic during an emotional crisis and are swept along with the counsel to abort their unborn child, only to be left with the guilt and torment of having taken a life.

What Are the Alternatives?

The only alternative to death is to let live.

The pregnant woman has guidelines from the Word of God, to help in her decision to value and care for the life that has been placed within her.

See, I have set before you today life and prosperity, and death and adversity. . . . I call heaven and earth to witness against you today, that I have set before you life and death, the blessing and the curse. So choose life in order that you may live, you and your descendants.

Deuteronomy 30:15, 19

Any woman struggling with the decision of whether to allow a life to continue or to destroy the life within her, has our great sympathy. It is women who have determined, before pregnancy occurs, that the simplest answer is to abort any inconvenient or unwanted pregnancies, that have our disgust and rejection because of their low value for human life. The woman who is trying to make a right choice should make use of one of the life-line agencies that will counsel her to "let live." There are many birth-control clinics and Planned Parenthood clinics available across the nation for free examinations and counsel, a good number of them undoubtedly recommending abortion as the only answer. However, there are numerous agencies ready and willing to aid the pregnant woman in giving life to her child, whether through financial, housing, or emotional support or medical services. Beyond that, they will assist by giving her hope and freedom from guilt, because she is being obedient to God's Word. (Confidential information will be given, regarding the address of a local agency, on writing to Concerned Women for America, P.O. Box 20376, El Cajon, California 92021.)

Turning from God's law and authority only compounds problems and creates new ones. When we put such little worth on human life that we can destroy it at will, it must grieve the heart of God. He valued it so greatly that He willingly gave His Son, Jesus Christ, to die, in order to save life. How far we have drifted from God's values and from His intended role for women: designed to give life, not to destroy it; designed to give a beautiful, added dimension to life, not to misuse it.

4
Subordinate, but Not Inferior

Women who feel stifled by the biblical teaching on submission have yet to understand the biblical meaning of freedom. Scripture repeatedly refers to a woman as a helper, an assistant, and a subordinate. The suggestion of this immediately turns some readers off, because they associate a subordinate with one who is inferior.

To fully understand the submissive role of the woman, it is necessary to ignore present-day usage of this word and concentrate on the biblical terms that accurately describe the relationship. If submission and subordination are defined by current usage, you arrive at terms such as *inferior, underling, slavish,* or *second-string.* Women need to recognize and accept the truth that God did not create them inferior. Therefore, submission does not arise from inferiority. In accordance with the consistency of Scripture, these modern terms must be discounted, and a further study must be made of biblical examples of subordination.

Patterns With a Purpose

One of the best ways to view submission or subordination, as it relates to scriptural teaching, is in reference to God's divine purpose and established order. David Nicholas gives an excellent summary of this relationship when he writes:

> In creation God established order, and the continuation of God's creation is dependent upon the things "created" following an orderly pattern—a pattern established by the "Creator." The cosmic bodies, for instance, must be in subjection to one another via the laws of gravity. Likewise, subatomic particles are programmed to follow the laws of attraction and repulsion in order to perpetuate the continued existence of atoms. One could not say that an electron is inferior to a proton or neutron, for each is vital to the makeup of the atom. Now, if God has established laws of order in the created universe, why then should it be surprising that He has established various roles for the men and women He created to fulfill in the home and the church? And why should any of His created human beings feel inferior when assigned a subordinate role? A subordinate role is many times just as important, or even more important, than a headship role.[1]

Jesus Sets the Example

In order for God to accomplish His divine purpose of providing redemption for sinful man, it was necessary for Christ to become subordinate to Almighty God. Christ was not inferior or less important than God the

Father in bringing to completion the plan for man's salvation. Submission, however, was necessary to provide for our salvation. Another example is clearly given by Paul, when he compares the subordination of woman to man with the subordination of Christ to God. "But I want you to understand that Christ is the head of every man, and the man is the head of a woman, and God is the head of Christ" (1 Corinthians 11:3).

Anything short of this kind of relationship among Christ, man, woman, and God is deficient in the divine order and plan for mankind. To say that God intended woman to be the inferior partner to man is accusing Christ of being second-rate to God the Father. Scripture proves that to be not so!

Just before Jesus was betrayed, arrested, taken before Pilate, and condemned to die on the cross, He went to the Mount of Olives to pray. As He began to agonize in prayer to the Father at the Garden of Gethsemane and to ask that the Father might remove the cup of sin from Him, He demonstrated the kind of submission that comes as a result of total obedience: "And He withdrew from them about a stone's throw, and He knelt down and began to pray, saying, 'Father, if Thou art willing, remove this cup from Me; yet not My will, but Thine be done' " (Luke 22:41, 42).

Headship Requires "Bodyship"

Jesus and the Father were both necessary to complete the death, burial, and Resurrection making sal-

vation possible for all who will accept this free gift of
eternal life.

Another passage in the Bible that reveals the importance of Jesus Christ in the plan of God is found in
Ephesians 1:

> that the God of our Lord Jesus Christ, the Father of
> glory, may give to you a spirit of wisdom and of reve-
> lation in the knowledge of Him. I pray that the eyes
> of your heart may be enlightened, so that you may
> know what is the hope of His calling, what are the
> riches of the glory of His inheritance in the saints,
> and what is the surpassing greatness of His power
> toward us who believe. These are in accordance
> with the working of the strength of His might
> which He brought about in Christ, when He raised
> Him from the dead, and seated Him at His right
> hand in the heavenly places, far above all rule and
> authority and power and dominion, and every name
> that is named, not only in this age, but also in the
> one to come. And He put all things in subjection
> under His feet, and gave Him as head over all
> things to the church, which is His body, the fulness
> of Him who fills all in all.
>
> Ephesians 1:17–23

Before Jesus Christ could be seated at the right
hand of God the Father and all things be made subject
under Him, as head over the Church, He first had to
be subordinate to God, in obedience to the divine plan.

So the wife is to be subordinate to the husband, in obedience to God's divine plan, not inferior or second-rate. "Wives, be subject to your own husbands, as to the Lord" (Ephesians 5:22).

Submission Is an Attitude

Submission is an attitude of obedience. True submission, which is motivated by a genuine desire to be obedient to the heavenly Father, makes no consideration of selfish ends. "What will I get in return, if I submit? Is he worthy of my submission? Will I lose my self-identity and my individual rights, if I submit to my husband?" Ephesians 5:22 says the wife is to submit to her own husband *as to the Lord*. Forget about the husband-wife association for a moment, and examine the scriptural teaching of a godly woman's submission to the Lord.

Before a woman can successfully submit to her husband, she must first submit to Christ. Submitting to the Lord means giving up all selfish desires and personal rights. We are told to be servants of Christ and to follow Him (John 12:24–26). The old self, with its corruption of selfish lusts and deceit, is to be laid aside, and we are to be renewed in the likeness of God, created in righteousness and holiness of the truth (Ephesians 4:22–24). No longer are we alone in our control of our direction and decisions, but the Holy Spirit is to superintend (or govern) our lives. That will ultimately affect our emotions, attitudes, responses,

reactions, and our total being (Ephesians 5:18–21).
This kind of selfless, God-filled living will enable a
woman to submit to her husband without fear of losing
her identity, individuality, or equality in the marriage
bonds.

The woman who is truly spirit-filled will want to be
totally submissive to her husband. Regardless of
what the current trend towards Women's Lib advocates, anything which departs from God's design for
women is not right. Submission does not mean that
she is owned and operated by her husband but that
he is the head or manager. A manager knows how
to develop and use the gifts in others. This is what
God intended the husband to do for the wife. He
helps her develop to her greatest potential. He
keeps track of the overall picture but puts her in
charge of areas where she functions well. This is a
truly liberated woman. Submission is God's design
for woman. Christ's example teaches that true submission is neither reluctant nor grudging, nor is it a
result of imposed authority; it is rather an act of
worship to God when it is a chosen, deliberate, vol-
untary response to a husband.[2]

Because submission is an attitude of obedience—
first to the Lord, then to her husband—a woman can
experience freedom and/or liberation through Christ.
"For you were called to freedom, brethren; only do not
turn your freedom into an opportunity for the flesh,

but through love serve one another" (Galatians 5:13).
Too often women campaign for more freedom in marriage, only to turn freedom into an opportunity for the flesh. Paul warns against such motives. With freedom through Christ, we are to have a servant's heart, filled with love.

Some of you are objecting, because you know of marriages where the women have been slaves to their husbands, or were treated as second-class citizens. That is sadly true, in some cases. Nevertheless, such a wrong does not alter the biblical teaching on submission to the Lord or a woman's submission to her husband. It is important to keep our eyes on what God teaches as the standard, and not on man's misuse of circumstances.

Paul and the ERA

In recent years many questions have been raised, by both men and women, about submission—justifiably so. Feminist voices are being heard from within churches, stating that the teaching of submitting to a husband is archaic and denotes the woman is inferior. They say it was right for Paul's day, but that Ephesians 5 allows for an evolution in the marriage relationship. After all, they continue, Paul's followers were influenced by the patriarchal structure of Israelite society. They continue to take the Pauline epistles and dissect them for their own benefit.

Most of the same people who are denouncing bibli-

cal submission are forceful supporters of the Equal
Rights Amendment. There is a strong tendency to use
enough Scripture to remain "spiritual" while explain-
ing away, or even omitting, the verses that conflict
with their personal opinions. Is it any wonder that
within sound, Bible-teaching churches, discordant
questions are being asked, regarding the true teachings on submission?

Wives are not the only ones told to submit to another. Ephesians 5:21 exhorts all believers to "be subject to one another in the fear of Christ." This teaches
that all members of the body of Christ are to submit to
one another, including wives to husbands and husbands to wives. It is this biblical principle that should
identify the family of God to the rest of the world: the
attitude of loving, caring for, and serving one another.
This kind of submission does not lead to self-destruction, nor does it mean one is inferior to another.
Rather, it enriches an individual's life and promotes
him to a more mature level, resulting in good self-esteem, loving concern for others, and a general attitude
of well-being. Why? Because such submission is an act
of obedience to our heavenly Father. Likewise, wife-to-
husband submission does not lead to self-destruction;
nor does it mean the wife is inferior to her husband.
Because it is a response in obedience to God, she will
have good self-esteem, loving concern for others, and a
general attitude of well-being.

Counterfeit Submission

It is possible to submit for selfish gain: "If I act submissive, then my husband will buy me what I want." Or, "I will get my own way, if I submit." A woman would rarely verbalize these thoughts, but her underlying motivation is for selfish gain or revenge. Then, if and when her husband does not respond in the direction she is trying to manipulate him, she turns off the submission (and sometimes the sex). Even Christian women can be motivated by these deceitful, selfish impulses.

This is not the kind of submission that Ephesians is discussing. Examine your reactions, and you will have a good indication of your motivation for submitting. See *Figure 2*.

SUBMISSION—GIVING OR GETTING		
Examples in Marriage	Spirit-Controlled Submission Is Giving	Self-Motivated Submission Is Getting
Act of Marriage Husband's Authority Finances Decision making Speech Hospitality Wife's Duties Spiritual Leadership Material Possessions	Regardless of the outcome, the reactions are: Loving Joyful Peaceful Patient Kind Goodness Faithful Gentle Self-control	When it does not get, the reactions are: Lustful Resentful Anxious Demanding Flattering Deceitful Slothful Nagging Greedy

Figure 2

God's Answer to Conflict

Submission has importance when two people disagree. Submission does not remove conflicting ideas or opinions in marriage—and should not. Husband and wife are individuals, with different temperaments, different personalities, different likes and dislikes, different backgrounds, and different opinions. If two people always agree, then one of them is no longer necessary. There will always be disagreements in marriage, but submission gives a married couple a way of resolving those conflicts. If submission is an attitude of loving, caring, serving each other, and being teachable, then, out of love, care, and a desire to serve her, the husband will be interested in considering the wife's opinions. He, too, is told to "submit one to another." In like manner, the wife will want to hear her husband's opposing views, because of the submissive spirit assigned to her as a wife and as a member of the Body of Christ.

The final decision can be made by God's appointed method. Ephesians 5:23 tells the husband to be the "head," or in authority, over the wife. Please remember, he has already been commanded, as a member of the family of God, to have a submissive spirit toward his wife. He has never been told to be the sole decision maker in the home. Because he is obedient to God and lovingly submits to his wife, he will want her to express her frustrations, anxieties, disappointments, and differing ideas. He will not respond to her as a domineering tyrant or as an army sergeant shouting out orders; nor will he respond as one husband, who proclaimed, "I'm not interested in what you think!" If he does, then he is not obedient to verse 21, which speaks of submitting to one another. He is God's appointed "submissive head" of the wife. Though these words may seem contradictory, they are not. Submission is assigned to all believers, even the husband, but he is also the appointed leader.

Full consideration should be given to both sides of the conflict, but when the time comes for making the final decision, the wife must commit her husband to Jesus Christ as he exerts his responsibility as the submissive head. When she has expressed all of her feelings, insights, emotions, and judgments on the subject, she can then ask her heavenly Father to give wisdom, direction, and the proper decision to her husband, as he fulfills his role.

When a husband uses his headship to justify authoritarian actions and attitudes, he is not acting in obedience to God. This is a sacred trust imparted to him, which must be handled with reverence and honor. Anything short of this is motivated by selfish opportunity and gratification of the flesh.

Husbands to Love

Husbands are told to love their wives, just as Christ loved the Church (Ephesians 5:25). Christ's love for the Church was sacrificial, even to the point of giving Himself up for her!

Husbands, love your wives, just as Christ also loved
the church and gave Himself up for her; that He
might sanctify her, having cleansed her by the
washing of water with the word, that He might present to Himself the church in all her glory, having
no spot or wrinkle or any such thing; but that she
should be holy and blameless. So husbands ought
also to love their own wives as their own bodies. He
who loves his own wife loves himself; for no one
ever hated his own flesh, but nourishes and
cherishes it, just as Christ also does the church.

Ephesians 5:25–29

When this kind of love and submission exist between husband and wife, then the matter of headship
or authority does not become a divisive issue. There
begins to be a spiritual blending and molding of minds
and wills, so that these two different individuals develop the attitude that is expressed in the New Testament:

If therefore there is any encouragement in Christ, if
there is any consolation of love, if there is any fellowship of the Spirit, if any affection and compassion, make my joy complete by being of the same
mind, maintaining the same love, united in spirit,
intent on one purpose. Do nothing from selfishness
or empty conceit, but with humility of mind let each
of you regard one another as more important than

himself; do not merely look out for your own personal interests, but also for the interests of others.

Philippians 2:1–4

Example of Christ Jesus

Probably the most beautiful example of God's ideal in the marriage relationship is found in the attitude of Christ, as we continue in Philippians:

Have this attitude in yourselves which was also in Christ Jesus, who, although He existed in the form of God, did not regard equality with God a thing to be grasped, but emptied Himself, taking the form of a bondservant, and being made in the likeness of men. And being found in appearance as a man, He humbled Himself by becoming obedient to the point of death, even death on a cross. Therefore also God highly exalted Him, and bestowed on Him the name which is above every name, that at the name of Jesus every knee should bow, of those who are in heaven, and on earth, and under the earth, and that every tongue should confess that Jesus Christ is Lord, to the glory of God the Father.

Philippians 2:5–11

From this Scripture, we see four distinct steps that Christ fulfilled. Just as Ephesians 5:22 tells a woman to submit to her husband in the same way that she submits to the Lord, such submission falls into four steps, which can be paralleled with Christ's example.

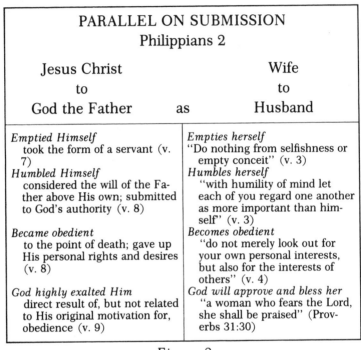

PARALLEL ON SUBMISSION
Philippians 2

Jesus Christ to God the Father	as	Wife to Husband
Emptied Himself took the form of a servant (v. 7) *Humbled Himself* considered the will of the Father above His own; submitted to God's authority (v. 8)		*Empties herself* "Do nothing from selfishness or empty conceit" (v. 3) *Humbles herself* "with humility of mind let each of you regard one another as more important than himself" (v. 3)
Became obedient to the point of death; gave up His personal rights and desires (v. 8)		*Becomes obedient* "do not merely look out for your own personal interests, but also for the interests of others" (v. 4)
God highly exalted Him direct result of, but not related to His original motivation for, obedience (v. 9)		*God will approve and bless her* "a woman who fears the Lord, she shall be praised" (Proverbs 31:30)

Figure 3

Does this sound too difficult? Yes, it is difficult, because our selfish nature wants to gain the most for the least. But this is a formula for the woman who wants to be Christlike. Down through the ages, volumes of books and reams of paper have been filled with writings on submission. There is nothing new to be said and still remain true to the Scripture. It simply boils down to a woman's total dedication to Jesus Christ, which surpasses her human goals and selfish motivations. When her strongest desire is to be absolutely yielded to the Holy Spirit and totally obedient to God's will, submission becomes a natural part of her life. In the final analysis, this life is just a passing moment, in light of eternity, and female equality and personal rights seem trivial and insignificant.

"For it is God who is at work in you, both to will and to work for His good pleasure" (Philippians 2:13).

5
Designed for Pleasure

The most beautiful, and yet the most misused, of all God's gifts to male and female alike is the potential for a sexual relationship with the marriage partner. I specifically limited it to marriage because God ordained sexual relations be confined within the bonds of marriage. It is the beautiful culmination of a partnership communion, expressed in the most intimate and satisfying of all relationships and designed for pleasure and enjoyment.

Harmful Attitudes

During the Victorian age, it was believed that a woman should never enjoy sex, and if she had a sex drive, she was a "loose woman." An excessive interest in the act of marriage on the part of the wife was sufficient cause for the husband to be suspicious. Unfortunately, remnants of this attitude have carried into the twentieth century, passed along from mother to daughter.

It is almost unbelievable, to read some of the ridiculous distortions to which the beautiful relationship of married love has been subjected. Letha Scanzoni writes:

Peter Lombard and Gratien warned Christians that the Holy Spirit left the room when a married couple engaged in sexual intercourse—even if it were for the purpose of conceiving a child! Other church leaders insisted that God required sexual abstinence during all holy days and seasons. And in addition, couples were advised not to have sex relations on Thursdays in honor of Christ's arrest, on Fridays in memory of His crucifixion, on Saturdays in honor of the Virgin Mary, on Sundays in remembrance of Christ's resurrection, and on Mondays out of respect for the departed souls (leaving only Tuesday and Wednesday)! The Church sought to regulate every facet of life, leaving no room for the individual's right to determine God's will, nor for the rights of a married couple to decide for themselves how the most intimate aspects of married life should be conducted.[1]

Fortunately, more Christians began to study the Word of God, following the Reformation. They discovered that God is the author of sex. God equipped male and female for the experience of married love and intended them to enjoy it.

The Christian Woman and Sex

Among Christian women, there are diverse attitudes toward sex, including dislike, endurance, fear, and shame. Others think of sex as an unpleasant duty or a necessary part of being submissive to one's husband. But God intended sex to be enjoyed by *both* husband and wife.

The Song of Solomon portrays a beautiful picture of husband and wife enjoying the physical pleasures of married love without guilt or shame. The utter delight that the bride has for the groom in the Song of Solomon is demonstrated by her excited participation in this adventure with her husband (Song of Solomon 4; 7). The story certainly suggests ample time was allowed for physical pleasure and enjoyment. There was no hurry, nor was there any shame. Somehow the false notion has been passed on that something as pleasurable and exciting as sex cannot be of God: Therefore, it must be sinful. However, this concept is inaccurate. The only time sex becomes sinful is when it is practiced contrary to God's standards of morality. God designed sex for married partners. Anything outside of that is a violation of God's law.

The Bible speaks out clearly against the misuse or abuse of sex, labeling it "adultery" or "fornication." The only prohibition on sex in the Scripture relates to extramarital or premarital activity. Without exception, the Bible is abundantly clear on that subject, condemning all such conduct.

Male and Female Differences

There is a concerted effort by the feminists to convince the public that the differences between men and women are solely biological. Radical feminists have vocally denounced other sexual differences and have declared that any distinction between the sexes is culturally and environmentally inspired. Dr. James Dobson strongly opposes this mistaken idea and states that males and females differ biochemically, anatomically, and emotionally. He continues by naming a few differences between men and women. Men carry a different chromosomal pattern than women. The emotional center provides women with a different psychological basis than men. Female sexual desire tends to be cyclical, while the sex drive in males is acyclical. Men are stimulated visually, and women are stimulated by the sense of touch. Sex for a woman is usually a deeply emotional experience, culminating in a feeling of warmth and affection. For men, it is strongly physical, leaving them exhausted and sleepy.[2] The differences are pronounced, and they must be recognized, to fully enjoy the ultimate pleasure God intended for the intimate act of marriage.

The Gift of Sex

God created every part of the human body. He did not create some parts good and others bad. He did not intend that certain parts of the human anatomy should be shameful. The equipping of male and female bodies with individualized organs for use in harmonic union was God's gift of sex to mankind. Mankind could never have thought of such a beautiful, intimate, and fulfilling relationship.

God's design for women goes beyond the roles of wife, mother, and companion. It includes her being a lover—a sexual partner in marriage—enjoying herself and experiencing pleasure. God, the Creator of sex, set human drives in motion not to torture men and women, but to bring them to completion and fulfillment. In our book *The Act of Marriage*, Tim and I state:

> Genesis 2 affords a more detailed description of God's creation of Adam and Eve, including the statement that God Himself brought Eve to Adam (v. 22), evidently to introduce them formally and give them the command to be fruitful. Then it beautifully describes their innocence in these words: "They were both naked, the man and his wife, and were not ashamed" (v. 25). Adam and Eve knew no embarrassment or shame on that occasion for three reasons: they were introduced by a holy and righteous God who commanded them to make love; their minds were not preconditioned to guilt, for no prohibitions concerning the act of marriage had yet been given; and no other people were around to observe their intimate relations.[3]

The gift of sex was intended to be used unselfishly. It was not given for selfish fulfillment, but for surrendering oneself completely to another. This requires consideration of the other person. To the Christian woman, the act of marriage is an extension of the art of submission: ". . . through love serve one another" (Galatians 5:13). On the other hand, the husband receives the same instruction—to lovingly serve his wife—in Ephesians 5:21.

Finally, the gift of sex was to be preserved for the one special person with whom the vow of marriage is shared. It was never meant to be abused, distorted, or adulterated, but was intended for the purposes of "filling the earth" (Genesis 1:28) and for "satisfying at all times" (Proverbs 5:18, 19). God's purpose and design for the male-and-female relationship was to be expressed in the beauty of married sexual love.

6
Is There a Place for Women in the Church?

Here is another subject encircled by great controversy—one that is a drum the Evangelical Women's Caucus beats continually. There are those who believe that Paul was wrong in his teachings on marriage and church leadership, while others deny that the Apostle Paul even wrote 1 Corinthians 14 and 1 Timothy. The issue at stake regards the limitations of what a woman can do in the Church. May she be ordained? May she serve communion? Are Church women today victims of tradition?

My desire and purpose is to relate all these questionable issues to the authority of the Scripture; that is the only unchanging truth. God does not contradict His principles. The conscientious Christian woman will be more concerned with the biblical teachings on this subject than she will with the secular, sociological pressures regarding these "rights" of women. No doubt Letha Scanzoni and Nancy Hardesty have contributed to this confusion over scriptural teaching through their writings regarding women in the Church. They are very adamant that women be al-

lowed to fill positions in the Church that previously
have been limited to men. Their argument continues:

> Overall, it is clear that while many people feel they
> are arguing on the basis of scriptural prohibitions,
> they are simply standing on theological tradition
> based on cultural prejudices. What they are saying
> is that for one sex, half the human race, sexual dif-
> ferentiation is a handicap so crippling that no
> amount of personal talent, intelligence, piety, or
> even divine enabling, can make them ministers of
> the gospel.[1]

If the qualifications for being a minister were personal talents or gifts, there would be no question concerning women being ordained for the ministry. Certainly there are many who would qualify for this profession under those standards. However, these two
authors have overlooked the scriptural instruction to
women.

The Bible's Unpopular Answer

The Bible's direct approach on many subjects has
not necessarily agreed with the majority opinion.
Many of the issues in question have been discussed in
this book, but another that needs to be added to the list
is the role of the woman in the Church.

The answer is not found in what the Presbyterians,
Methodists, Catholics, Baptists, or Pentecostals teach;

nor is it what the feminists, Christian or otherwise, are advocating. The basis must be what the Word of God says about women in the Church.

Paul has uniquely drawn a comparison between the husband-wife relationship and that of Christ and His bride, the Church (Ephesians 5:22–33). Without belaboring this principle, the passage briefly says that wives are subject to husbands, just as the Church is subject to Christ. The Church and the wife are interchangeable in this example, as are Christ and the husband. Christ and the husband are heads of the Church and the wife respectively (v. 23), and Christ is the head of every man (1 Corinthians 11:3). Paul concedes that this is a great mystery (Ephesians 5:32); it is a "heavenly truth," to be enacted in the Christian home and the Church. Male and female are "one in Christ" (Galatians 3:28), and yet the man is the head of the woman (1 Corinthians 11:3), another facet of the great mystery.

When this truth is denied, it destroys the fundamental teaching of Ephesians 5. If the argument is valid that the man should not be the head of the woman, then Christ should not be the head of the Church. God forbid!

This leads to the question under discussion: Should sociological trends be allowed to dictate Church policy concerning woman's role in the Church? The movement for women's rights is attempting to revolutionize the Church, insisting that Church policy regarding the status of women be changed. The forerunners of

the Evangelical Women's Caucus strongly proclaim
that women should be ordained ministers, leading
local churches. Let us examine the contributions
made by a few of the female workers in the early
Church of the apostolic age.

Women Who Served

Women throughout history have had a vital part in
the local church—not in the leadership, but always in
the ministry of service. Paul apparently admired the
women church workers and considered them his
friends and co-laborers, because he mentions them
many times. Romans 16 is Paul's record of special recognition given to twenty-four servants of Christ, six of
whom are women. William Barclay comments on this
list:

> Of the twenty-four, six are women. That is worth re-
> membering, for often Paul is accused of belittling
> the status of women in the church. If we really wish
> to see Paul's attitude toward women in the church,
> it is a passage like this that we should read, where
> his appreciation of the work that they were doing in
> the church shines and glows through his words.[2]

Women were involved in many diverse areas of
ministry. A partial list follows:

Hospitality   Lydia (Acts 16:15, 40) opened her
home as a base for outreach and discipleship. Nympha

(Colossians 4:15) opened her home for church meetings.

Gift of Helps   Phoebe (Romans 16:1, 2) was called a "servant of the church." Dorcas (Acts 9:36) abounded with deeds of kindness and charity, which she performed continually.

Workers (not much detail mentioned)   Mary (Romans 16:6) worked hard for the church. Tryphaena and Tryphosa (Romans 16:12) were probably sisters who worked hard for the Lord.

Prophesying   Four daughters of Philip (Acts 21:8, 9) were "virgins who were prophetesses."

Teaching   Priscilla (Acts 18:26; Romans 16:3) taught the way of God with her husband. She was called a fellow worker in Christ Jesus.

Each of these women was working under the leadership and authority of local churches led by men. They were functioning with their gifts, yet still in obedience to Jesus Christ. In the Church, authority is in the hands of men because they represent Christ and the great mystery. If you disagree, you are rebelling against Christ's authority as head of the Church.

The ultimate goal of the total ministry of the Church is to introduce people to Christ and to teach them the Word of God for their spiritual growth. This area of service is open to every Christian, male *and* female; in fact, we are all commanded to be witnesses of Christ.

If the desire of women who campaign for female ordination is that they might be able to win others to Christ and teach the Word, this is already commanded. A person does not need ordination papers to lead a person to Christ or to teach a Bible study. However, if the motivation involves a desire for leadership over a congregation, then it becomes a selfish desire for an elevated position. The Bible gives the man that responsibility in the Church, as Christ's representative.

Scripturally, women can serve as deacons (deaconesses) in the local church (1 Timothy 3:10, 11). Though the requirements for deacons are listed in the masculine, the passage indicates that women who are deacons must also abide by definite standards. Phoebe was a deaconess (Romans 16:1), for a deaconess is one who serves the needs of the congregation. However, women are not to serve as elders (overseers or ministers). Scripture does not continue with a "likewise" for women, in regard to the office of a minister.

"It is a trustworthy statement; if any *man* aspires to the office of overseer, it is a fine work *he* desires to do. An overseer, then, must be above reproach, the *husband* of one wife . . ." (1 Timothy 3:1, 2 *italics mine*).

Female Submission to the Church

Just as women are exhorted to be submissive to their husbands at home, they are also to be under the authority of the minister of their local church. This is true of single women as well. *All* Christian women are to be in an attitude of submission, both at home and at church.

This is not a popular teaching, because the female's mind is being programmed to demand her rights, regardless of whether she is at home or at church. The feminist revolution is even affecting attitudes regarding scriptural truths. A reminder of the instructions from 2 Peter may help the Christian woman take her eyes off the sociological trends and return to the truth in the Word:

You therefore, beloved, knowing this beforehand, *be on your guard* lest, being carried away by the error of unprincipled men, you fall from your own steadfastness, but grow in the grace and knowledge of our Lord and Savior Jesus Christ. . . ."

2 Peter 3:17, 18, *italics mine*

Our growth is to be in the "grace and knowledge of our Lord Jesus Christ," not in our personal rights as women. Using human reason to persuade people that the status of women in the Church promotes inequality does not alter the fact that this truth is beyond human understanding. It is a heavenly truth. Just as Paul said, it is a great mystery. Therefore we must accept it, trusting the Almighty God, who designed us for a definite purpose.

Women Who Teach

The Scripture does not say that women cannot teach, as some would have us believe. It does, however, put limitations on the woman who teaches. She is not to teach or preach in the church services (1 Corinthians 14:34). This passage in 1 Corinthians contains instructions for the organized Church and its services. She is not to teach in church without her husband's permission, and is never to usurp his authority (1 Timothy 2:11, 12). While wives may teach Bible classes, Sunday schools, seminars, and so forth, they are not to speak without having their husbands' approval and being under his authority. In the case of a single woman or an absentee husband, the minister is to be the figure of authority.

In my ministry with my husband, I have occasionally been asked to justify my speaking to a mixed audience in a Family Life Seminar. This has only been done as a result of much prayer and careful scrutiny of Scripture, because God's hand of blessing on my life is more important to me than the opportunity to minister. Because my ministry is in accordance with the scriptural conditions set forth, I have the freedom to continue with God's blessing. First of all, I am always under the authority and approval of my husband when I speak. Secondly, a seminar is not an organized church service, and was never intended to be conducted as such; it is similar to a classroom teaching situation. Thirdly, as my husband often says, he has asked me to share the seminar program with him, and I am following his instructions.

I am careful, however, not to accept speaking engagements during a regularly scheduled church service, particularly the Sunday-morning worship service. On a few occasions, I have shared a report during a Sunday-night family service, but always with my husband or the local minister in full charge of the meeting.

Whose Rights Should We Consider?

So much emphasis has been put on a woman's individual rights that we have strayed from the most important issue: God is the controller of a Christian's life. The whole meaning of the Christian faith is dying to self and living in Christ. When Christ takes control of a life, rights and selfish desires are yielded to His divine authority. The question is no longer what is being given up, but what is being gained through Christ. It is not the Church that needs to fit in with the world's sociological changes; rather, the world needs to conform to the teachings of *Jesus Christ!*

7
Distinctive in Being a Woman

The Bible is a practical guidebook for living, giving us instruction on proper attitudes in conducting our daily affairs. Most principles are written, in general, to all Christians, but some are sorted out and directed toward women, just as others are directed toward men. Few of the distinctions mentioned on the following pages are repeated for male instruction.

Women of all ages, whether single, married, or widowed, are included in the biblical principles for developing a godly woman. The basic foundation for all of these instructions is the fundamental teaching that the Lord desires all people, male and female, to come to repentance. In other words, everyone needs to receive Jesus Christ as Lord and Saviour. "But as many as received Him, to them He gave the right to become children of God, even to those who believe in His name" (John 1:12). This step requires confession of all sin to Jesus Christ and inviting Him to take control, to become Lord and Saviour. "For whoever will call upon the name of the Lord will be saved" (Romans 10:13). The only way a person can have his sins forgiven and become part of the family of God is to call on the Lord for salvation. God's family is a combination of both males and females.

Instructions to Christian Women

The Bible makes a definite distinction between the sexes. Christ died for the sins of all and gave instructions for our spiritual growth. However, to clarify the different roles and purposes for the male and female, there are some passages of Scripture that speak only to women and others that speak only to men. If God intended us to be a unisex society, He would have written a unisex Bible for our instruction.

As we examine a few of the verses that speak to women, do not be discouraged if you fall short of fulfilling the requirements. A person cannot decide to change and immediately forget the old ways, suddenly becoming an example of the Spirit-filled believer. Success in all circumstances and stages of life is dependent upon walking in the Spirit. One can decide, however, to begin immediately to allow the Holy Spirit to control her attitudes, actions, and abilities (Romans 8:5). This is yielding the selfish will to the will of the heavenly Father.

Properly Adorned

"Likewise, I want women to adorn themselves with proper clothing, modestly and discreetly, not with braided hair and gold or pearls or costly garments" (1 Timothy 2:9).

"And let not your adornment be external *only*—

braiding the hair, and wearing gold jewelry, and putting on dresses" (1 Peter 3:3).

This subject has been belabored in many books, but it is important to mention it again, because it has a direct correlation to a woman's godly living. God does not denounce beauty; He simply wants it to be kept in the right order of priority. Paul did not say it is wrong to wear gold, pearls, or clothing. He is telling women not to allow external things to be their criteria for beauty. True beauty comes from within. Modesty must begin with a woman's attitude, after which it will manifest itself in her dress and demeanor, including control of the body, its movements and impulses. When the attitude is self-controlled and disciplined, the adorning of the body will be discreet, with care and caution, so that the outward adorning matches the inward attitude. Modesty includes respect for the feelings of others, and particularly for those of the male gender. It is an inadequate argument to claim that lust is the problem of the male. The Bible instructs women to show concern for them by being modestly adorned. *Discreetly* refers to controlling personal desires and not seeking to satisfy them through external adornment.

Gentle and Quiet Spirit

"But let it be the hidden person of the heart, with the imperishable quality of a gentle and quiet spirit, which is precious in the sight of God" (1 Peter 3:4). Our adornment is not to be *merely* external, but should also include adorning the hidden person of the heart. The internal dressing is a gentle and quiet spirit. The gentle spirit is not exclusively for women. When Jesus was teaching the multitudes, He said, "Blessed are the gentle, for they shall inherit the earth" (Matthew 5:5). The believer is instructed to walk in "all humility and gentleness" (Ephesians 4:2).

When a gentle and quiet spirit is demonstrated, the internal beauty becomes attractive to others and is precious in the sight of God. A consistently quiet spirit represents tranquillity from within. There is no dissension or hostility toward others. This characteristic is rarely seen among the feminist leaders: They exude hostility and bitterness. Christian women need to guard their hearts against this kind of reaction. It is contrary to what pleases God.

The gentle spirit, or meekness, as Christ referred to it, alludes to the attitude that accepts God's dealings with us as good and refuses to argue or take revenge on other people. This is contrary to our natural, sinful manner; therefore, it must be a result of the Holy Spirit controlling a woman's life. It is, in fact, included in the list of the fruits of the Spirit (Galatians 5:22, 23). Is it any wonder that this attitude is precious to God? The gentle and quiet spirit is a measure of a woman's God-related nature, not her natural disposition. It is revealed in the tone of her voice, her attitudes, her tongue, her compassion, and even in her manner of communication.

This attitude is more than just a cultural condition of Paul's day. It is another of the differences God created between the male and female. A loud, boisterous, sarcastic, and insensitive woman is hardly a display of femininity or internal beauty.

Submissive to Husband

"For in this way in former times the holy women also, who hoped in God, used to adorn themselves, being submissive to their own husbands" (1 Peter 3:5).

"For in this way" refers to the method for proper adornment previously discussed: modesty and discretion. Notice these women were called "holy women, who hoped in God." I don't know how many readers can identify with this statement, but I certainly want to be known as a holy woman who hopes in God. This is a portion of the growing process for becoming a godly woman. In addition to the proper adornment, verse 5 says godly women are submissive to their own husbands. Even the early women of God were obedient to Ephesians 5:22. Much more has been said on this subject in chapter 4. Let me encourage you to reread it, if you are struggling to accept this biblical principle.

Older Women to Be Reverent in Behavior, so They Can Teach the Young Women

"Older women likewise are to be reverent in their behavior, not malicious gossips, nor enslaved to much wine, teaching what is good" (Titus 2:3).

There is no distinction of age in this reference to an older woman. This could refer to older in physical age or, as some suggest, in spiritual age. A combination of the two would be a safe conclusion. Keep in mind, however, that a year is older than a month, and five years is older than one year. This means that as a person's spiritual growth begins, there will always be someone younger who needs teaching and help. It is important also to remain teachable; there are always those who are older and wiser. Each person is somewhere on the ladder of spiritual generations.

The instruction from this verse indicates that spiritual growth will be reflected in a person's behavior and way of life. We are told to be reverent, or worthy of respect, in order to set a good example for the younger women who need to be taught.

Not malicious gossips (1 Timothy 3:11). This is an instruction to all: The tongue must be guarded, to stay out of trouble. "He who guards his mouth and his tongue, Guards his soul from troubles" (Proverbs 21:23). "Let no unwholesome word proceed from your mouth. . ." (Ephesians 4:29). "He who goes about as a slanderer reveals secrets, Therefore do not associate with a gossip" (Proverbs 20:19). "And the tongue is a fire, the very world of iniquity; the tongue is set among our members as that which defiles the entire body, and sets on fire the course of our life, and is set on fire by hell" (James 3:6).

A teacher who is a malicious gossip or has a forked tongue is simply blowing into the wind as she teaches. The tongue needs to be tamed, so that she might be used of the Lord.

Women have a reputation for demonstrating a gossipy tongue. Perhaps that is why this sin was singled out for a specific instruction to women of old. There are numerous verses that emphasize the proper use of the tongue:

For I am afraid that perhaps when I come I may find you to be not what I wish and may be found by you to be not what you wish; that perhaps there may be strife, jealousy, angry tempers, disputes, slanders, gossip, arrogance, disturbances.

2 Corinthians 12:20

But now you also, put them all aside: anger, wrath, malice, slander, and abusive speech from your mouth.

Colossians 3:8

And just as they did not see fit to acknowledge God any longer, God gave them over to a depraved mind, to do those things which are not proper, being filled with all unrighteousness, wickedness, greed, mal-

ice; full of envy, murder, strife, deceit, malice; they
are gossips, slanderers, haters of God, insolent, ar-
rogant, boastful, inventors of evil, disobedient to
parents, without understanding, untrustworthy,
unloving, unmerciful.

Romans 1:28–31

God must have considered and wanted us to realize
how deadly are the sins of gossip and slander. Listing
them with those things that are not proper and result
from a depraved mind lends clarity to God's view on
the misuse of the tongue.

Nor enslaved to much wine (Titus 2:3). The unanswered question is, "How much wine is too much?"
There have been pages written on this subject. Some
feel strongly that the Bible teaches Christians should
abstain from wine or liquor. Others feel that moderate
amounts of wine are allowable, and they dabble in
what they personally determine is not "much wine."

It is very interesting that the secular world today
expects the dedicated Christian to be a nondrinker.
When a Christian takes a glass of wine or liquor with a
non-Christian, it dulls the sharp edge of his testimony
for Christ. My husband and I have been in the ministry of a local church for over thirty-three years. We
have watched scores of Christians, who argued that
the Bible approves of wine in moderation, make a de-
termination of what moderation was for them. We
have observed many of these fall by the wayside
through gradual disinterest. We cannot prove that

wine was the only problem, but it is interesting that we cannot name one Christian who has dabbled in drinking wine in moderation and maintained an active witness for Christ over a prolonged period of time. If there is a slim chance that a little wine could be wrong, it is preferable to be safe, rather than sorry, and abstain completely. My relationship to Jesus Christ is far more valuable than an occasional glass of wine. I am reminded of what the angel told Zacharias about John the Baptist—the son that Elizabeth would bear for him. The characteristics of importance that the angel shared were: He would be great in the sight of the Lord; he would drink no wine or liquor; he would be filled with the Holy Spirit; he would turn many to the Lord (Luke 1:15, 16).

I would encourage any woman who desires to be godly, and an effective teacher of that which is good, to ask the Lord to help her maintain the same four characteristics or standards set forth for John the Baptist.

Encourage the young women to love their husbands (Titus 2:4). Many times the Bible commands the husband to love his wife. That love is *agape,* or love that continues regardless of feelings (or lack of them). The love in Titus 2:4 is a *phileo* love, which is an emotionally responsive love. It is a love that is expressed with joy and delight—an enthusiastic love.

Gene Getz comments, "Paul made it very clear in this passage that this training process involved older women. The younger women needed a model, an example, a pattern. They needed to 'see' and 'experience' older women demonstrating loyalty, affection, and commitment to their husbands. They needed to learn how to love."[1]

The very word *teach,* or *encourage,* indicates that there is something to learn. In this instance. it is addressed to young women who need *to learn* to love their husbands. It is a response that requires work. Real, continuing love does not come easily or naturally; it involves a commitment that outlasts disagreements and conflicts.

Could it be that the older women have not faithfully taught the young women to love their husbands? The fact that the divorce rate is increasing so rapidly is indicative of the fact that young men and women have not *learned* how to love with a lasting commitment.

The attitude today is: Try it; if it does not work out, it was not meant to be. The first major controversy usually brings the conclusion that the relationship will not work. It is not too difficult to understand why Paul gave such an unusual instruction to the older ladies: The old and young alike bear the responsibility of making marriages last.

To love their children (Titus 2:4). This reference to love our children is about a friendly love, indicating fondness for one's child. The implication is that we should like them as people.

Once again, the instruction is to the older women: Encourage the young women to love their children— or be friendly and fond of them. This is also something that a mother needs to work on. It may help to visualize your children for what they are becoming, not what they are at the present. Every child goes through clumsy, awkward stages, which are tiresome and aggravating. Parental love can help him through these rough times, when he doesn't even like himself. It is important to maintain a positive attitude toward your children; they see themselves as they perceive you see them.

Psalms 113:9 talks about the "joyful mother of children." The term *mother* in the Hebrew relates to the "bond of the family"—the one who binds the family together. How necessary it is for a mother to learn to love her children, so the family might reap the results of her love.

The changing trends in our society insist that children can be raised just as well, if not better, in a child-care center as at home. After all, the government-supported and controlled child-care centers are led by professionals who know, even better than parents, how to raise children. It is this type of secular, humanistic philosophy that displays how little value is really placed on children and the home. I would challenge anyone to prove that the child-care center can provide the child with the same "bonding" that the Bible attributes to the mother alone. That is the missing dimension that cannot be replaced.

It would be unfair to say that all children whose mothers stay at home with them have better training than children whose mothers work. I have seen cases, on both sides of the issue, where the children have been disobedient, disrespectful, and certainly rebellious, just as I know families of both types that have produced delightful and responsible children. Some mothers have the capacity to be joyful mothers of children and give the added dimension of binding the family together while they are carrying on a position in the world of business. Other mothers find their energy is totally used up in mothering, and they cannot consider working outside the home.

The priority here is to see that, as a parent, you do not give your children leftovers of mom and dad in the evening. As parents, you teach by example the reactions and loving consideration they should have for one another. If you are worn-out from a day's work and short on patience, the same responses will be reflected in the children.

To go further, it is the parents' responsibility to teach their children the morals, values, and beliefs that are held by the family, thus giving them a closer bond as a family unit.

Loving your children includes responsibility for their total development—physical, moral, emotional, social, and spiritual. The older women are to encourage the younger women in this kind of love toward their children. Generations to come will reap the benefits of this kind of friendly bonding of families.

To be sensible, pure (Titus 2:5). In other words, this verse refers to self-control; it relates to a person who is sober and of a sound mind. Second Timothy 1:7 (KJV) states, "For God hath not given us the spirit of fear; but of power, and of love, and of a sound mind." All women can be sensible, with God's help. He has promised to give us a sound mind, if that is what we desire from Him. *Sound mind* describes a woman who is in control of her physical, psychological, and spiritual faculties. She is not in bondage to her desires, impulses, and passions.

Purity is expected of a Christian woman. Knowing Jesus Christ as Saviour should bring significant changes in a woman's life-style, particularly in the area of moral values. First Corinthians 6:18 states: "Flee immorality. Every other sin that a man commits is outside the body, but the immoral man sins against his own body."

This instruction is a challenge to maintain a pure heart. The Psalmist has said, "Create in me a clean heart, O God, And renew a steadfast spirit within me. Do not cast me away from Thy presence, And do not take Thy Holy Spirit from me" (Psalms 51: 10, 11).

God is the only source for help in having a pure heart. It is the presence of the Holy Spirit in us that enables us to be clean and pure. He directs our thoughts and actions and fills our minds with those things that produce clean hearts.

"Finally, brethren, whatever is true, whatever is honorable, whatever is right, whatever is pure, whatever is lovely, whatever is of good repute, if there is any excellence and if anything worthy of praise, let your mind dwell [meditate, think] on these things" (Philippians 4:8). When we, as women, think on purity, the actions those thoughts produce will be pure and clean. "He who has clean hands and a pure heart [our actions and our thoughts], Who has not lifted up his soul to falsehood, And has not sworn deceitfully. He shall receive a blessing from the Lord and righteousness from the God of his salvation" (Psalms 24:4, 5). What a promise of reward for obedience!

It is no wonder that the older women are told to encourage the young women to be sensible and pure. They, too, can receive blessings from the Lord.

Workers at home (Titus 2:5). This list becomes more controversial as we progress, but if it is your honest desire to know the biblical teachings for a woman, you will continue reading.

In checking the Greek for this phrase, I found that it means "keeper of the home," "domestically inclined," and "good housekeeper." The philosophy of the women's-rights movement has been in direct opposition to this biblical teaching. The feminist ideology is based entirely on a selfish orientation, encouraging a woman to look out for her own self-interests and rights. In a recent TV interview involving Betty Friedan, several women were questioned regarding their staying at home. One woman, after ten years of homemaking, decided she was trapped and had to be let out of her cage. Her solution was a 3–11 A.M. job as a taxi driver. After three years, she was still miserable and searching for the vacuum in her life to be filled. She will go on searching and never finding the peace and contentment she longs for until she meets Jesus

Christ and changes her self-orientation and interests to a spirit of giving and caring for others.

The Bible teaches just the opposite: "Do nothing from selfishness or empty conceit, but with humility of mind let each of you regard one another as more important than himself" (Philippians 2:3). In Galatians 5:13, Paul gives the biblical principle that true freedom results in serving one another in love. A woman who is subjected to the home, we are told, has been denied her right and privilege to get out of the house and develop her own career and self-interests. I reject the feminist philosophy that belittles a woman who chooses to stay at home, calling her a "trapped housewife."

The issue becomes a matter of priorities. True, a woman can develop interests outside of the home, but her top priority should and must be her home and family (*see* chapter 8). Each woman must evaluate how much she can handle outside the home without jeopardizing the quality time she should spend in being a good keeper of the home. This includes the keeping and bonding of the children, in which the age of the children is a vital factor. The younger they are, the more time they need in mother's company.

These verses in Titus 2 are speaking directly to women, old and young alike. It is women who are instructed to keep the home and bond the children together. I am not advocating that a wife become a slave to the home, rather that she is the director of home management, bearing the responsibility for its care and upkeep and the nurturing of children.

There is no mention of changing the roles of husband and wife; however, because a husband loves his wife, he is certainly encouraged to help her. There are great advantages for the husband who lends a hand with the children. This time gives him close contact with them and shows them that he can lovingly serve them, also. The husband who will not do the dishes, change a diaper, or scrub the floor, simply because he is a man, is acting in selfish arrogance and certainly is not supported by Scripture. Today the term "househusband" applies to the man who has agreed to reverse roles with his wife and remain at home to raise the children and do the homemaking. It would be rather interesting to peek inside that home in five or ten years, to determine the success and effectiveness of "househusbands."

It is possible today for a woman to be a businesswoman, a deaconess in her church, and a submissive wife at home, depending on her energy level. However, in order to fulfill these successfully, she must be able to keep her priorities in proper line. (She may also need to take extra vitamins.) This is assuming that this ambitious woman has no little children at home. If she has preschool children, it might be wise for her to wait a few years, until they are older and past their early developmental stage. Her home, husband, and children should always be her number-one priority. Titus tells the older women to encourage the younger women (most likely, mothers of young children) to stay at home and be homemakers. The older women have already experienced staying with children as a priority. Now they are told to encourage the young women to follow this same example. The famous woman in Proverbs 31 was certainly an active and productive lady. She was involved in projects in her home, community, and far away, but everything she engaged in was centered around the benefit of her family. She was a "keeper of the home."

I am sensitive to the fact that a home may consist of just one parent, who must be employed outside the home. This parent has no choice in the matter. The mother or father, whichever the case may be, must do triple duty in keeping the home, loving the children, and providing the needs of the family. Again, it is important to keep priorities in proper perspective. The time that is spent at home should be of the greatest quality for the children. During their waking hours at home with the parent, there can be activity and productivity. An organized method of cooperating in making dinner, doing dishes, laundry, and so forth, can be productive and rewarding to both parent and child. It takes careful planning and a proper attitude; there is no room for self-pity or a martyr complex. Make the best of the situation, and face it with the joyful contentment provided by the Holy Spirit to all who yield their problems to Him.

Encourage the young women to be kind (Titus 2:5). The new King James Bible uses the word *good* instead of "kind." Being kind would certainly result in deeds of goodness. Kindness is an attitude of concern for others, rather than for self. "And be kind to one another, tender-hearted, forgiving each other, just as God in Christ also has forgiven you" (Ephesians 4:32). This is really the opposite of *"deeds* that are of the flesh." We find kindness listed in the fruit of the Spirit in Galatians 5:22: "But the fruit of the Spirit is love, joy, peace, patience, kindness. . . ." These are attitudes which are not immediately visible; they begin to be reflected as we walk in the Spirit.

Subject to their own husbands (Titus 2:5). Once again women are told to be obedient to their own husbands (referring to chapter 4). This instruction seems to be discussed every time specific guidance is given to women. Its importance must derive from the fact that obedience is the measure of a woman's spirituality. All spiritual growth results in "less of self and more for others." This is true of the wife's relationship to her husband; it is a direct parallel to her relationship to Christ.

Attitudes of the flesh are difficult to fake. True obedience is clearly seen in a Spirit-filled life. The older women are instructed to encourage the young women in this biblical principle.

Word of God Not Dishonored

The distinct instructions to women in the Bible will result in bringing honor or dishonor to the Word of

God. This summary of Titus 2:3–5 is easily outlined as follows:

Older women instructed to:

1. Be reverent in the way they live
2. Not gossip or slander
3. Not be wine drinkers
4. Be teachers of what is good
5. Encourage the young women to:
   a. Love their husbands
   b. Love their children
   c. Be sensible
   d. Be pure
   e. Be workers at home
   f. Be kind
   g. Be subject to their own husbands

Why? ". . . that the word of God may not be dishonored" (Titus 2:5). We are expected to live in a manner that is above reproach, so that we will not bring dishonor or criticism to the Word of God.

Titus 2:7, 8 says, "In all things show yourself to be an example of good deeds, with purity in doctrine, dignified, sound in speech which is beyond reproach, in order that the opponent may be put to shame, having nothing bad to say about us."

8
The Modern Woman—Fulfilled or Frustrated as Homemaker?

Occupation: Housewife results in a full gamut of emotional responses, including everything from sheer delight and contentment, to call of duty and endurance, to resentment and frustration. I have observed countless women responding to questionnaires. As they reached the line asking for their occupation, there were those who did not hesitate, the rhythm of their pen continuing with the immediate response, "Homemaker." There were others who lingered and hesitated, perhaps trying to think of a more sophisticated term, and still others who skipped the line, either to return later or ignore it altogether.

Why is there such a hesitancy by so many to be labeled a housewife or homemaker? Perhaps a great deal of the confusion can be attributed to a misunderstanding of the full meaning of the term *homemaker*, as I prefer to call it.

Meaning of Homemaker

Homemaking is the art of making a home for the members of a family. It is the managing and upkeep of the habitation for loved ones and the providing of an atmosphere of hospitality, warmth, and security. It includes the care and training of the children. The homemaker sets the attitude and environment for all members of the family, including the husband. She contributes to their physical, emotional, mental, and spiritual needs and development.

All too often, homemaking is referred to as mundane tasks, such as changing diapers, mopping up spilled milk, and doing laundry. Those duties are necessary, but certainly are not the highest goals of homemaking. Every profession and occupation has its trivia, to which someone must attend. The business executive has office difficulties—such as personnel conflicts, space allotment, power struggles, and so forth—that cannot be ignored. But the executive does not place those necessary duties as the top priority or ultimate goal for being in the business world. If that were the only reward for the profession, he or she would undoubtedly seek another.

This seems to be the root of the problem, when confronting homemaking as a career. The emphasis has been placed on the necessary trivia, instead of on the ultimate goals and final result of shaping human lives that will affect future society. Dissatisfaction comes from dwelling on the inconsequential and losing sight of the unselfish, paramount target. The feminist leaders have contributed to this feeling by using such phrases as "the trivia of housewifing" or "the trapped housewife." Many of those who have responded to the call of the feminists have been victimized by an improper emphasis on the role of homemaker.

If a woman views only the labor of homemaking, then she will have ample cause for resentment and martrydom. This attitude is reflected in the illustration from *The Feminine Mystique*, by Betty Friedan:

> In Minneapolis recently a schoolteacher named Maurice K. Enghausen read a story in the local newspaper about the long work week of today's housewife. Declaring in a letter to the editor that "any woman who puts in that many hours is awfully slow, a poor budgeter of time, or just plain inefficient," this thirty-six-year-old bachelor offered to take over any household and show how it could be done.
>
> Scores of irate housewives dared him to prove it. He took over the household of Mr. and Mrs. Robert Dalton, with four children, aged two to seven, for three days. In a single day, he cleaned the first floor, washed three loads of clothes and hung them out to dry, ironed all the laundry including underwear and sheets, fixed a soup-and-sandwich lunch and a big backyard supper, baked two cakes, prepared two salads for the next day, dressed, undressed and bathed the children, washed woodwork and

scrubbed the kitchen floor. Mrs. Dalton said he was even a better cook than she was. "As for the cleaning," she said, "I am more thorough, but perhaps that is unnecessary."

Pointing out that he had kept house for himself for seven years and had earned money at college by housework, Enghausen said, "I still wish that teaching 115 students were as easy as handling four children and a house . . . I still maintain that housework is not the interminable chore that women claim it is."[1]

Even though Mr. Enghausen proved that he could handle the labor of homemaking for three days, I would question his effectiveness at molding and shaping the lives of the four Dalton children, on the schedule he was keeping. He apparently paid little attention to them, either emotionally or physically. Other than preparing their food, dressing, undressing, and bathing them, it seems they were deprived of the undivided attention they needed from a mother numerous times during the day. The four children were listed as ages two to seven. I would like to ask Mr. Enghausen if he had time to rock the two-year-old when it was needed, or to settle the arguments of the other children. Did he bandage the cut knees and give enough tender, loving care to stop the crying? Did he take time to shut off the iron and teach a lesson on lying that was needed at that very moment? Was he able to restore one child's self-image after a neighborhood child had all but destroyed it? What about time to answer the curious child, who was asking where babies come from? Were there moments for reading a story to the one who felt unloved and left out, and most important of all, was there time to answer questions about God and life and death?

Yes, full-blown homemaking is more than accomplishing a specific amount of cleaning in one day. It does include the labor. But more important than cleanliness is the molding and shaping of a young child's tender life. That cannot be classified as trivial, nor does it represent being trapped. It portrays a high calling and privilege not replaced by any other occupation or profession in the world.

Homemaking Fatigue

As in all demanding professions that are not limited by an eight-hour-day work schedule, the result can be extreme fatigue. No doubt an obstetrician experiences the weariness brought on by irregular work hours and the call of duty both day and night. This does not mean that he dislikes his job or is bored with it. It does indicate that he is human and his body is warning him of the need for rest, both mental and physical.

There is a different kind of fatigue, stimulated by boredom and inactivity. The homemaker who feels there is no challenge to the art of homemaking may experience an unexplainable fatigue. This should not be condemned. It may be that she is very well organized and her children are in school or gone from home, enabling her to finish her work around the house in one or two hours, leaving the remaining hours for boredom or lack of challenge. By night, she is worn out from doing little or nothing. There is also the woman who hates housework so much that she is tired before she starts. Admittedly, there are numerous cases of "housewife's fatigue" that are a result of boredom and inactivity. Sometimes the mother of one child will experience a greater fatigue than the woman with four or five children. It is not necessarily always boredom—it may result from physical differences in women.

A person's attitude toward a job can play an important role in how she feels physically. Facing homemaking with resentment will almost certainly produce fatigue. Philippians 4:6, 7 explains that when we approach everything with prayer and thanksgiving, the *peace* of God (contented spirit) will fill our hearts and minds. The thoughts and attitudes of your heart and mind will affect your sense of restlessness and boredom or peace and contentment. Does this spiritual truth have anything to do with homemaking? It most certainly does. The Christian woman has this divine source to aid her in accepting God's design for her as a woman. She can be a peaceful, contented homemaker, if that is God's will for her and if her attitude is in keeping with a thanksgiving spirit.

This does not mean that a woman was designed

solely for doing housework. That would be a false conclusion and equivalent to saying that a man is never to
assist his wife and should always be on the receiving
end of her services. Christians are told to "manage
well" their time. Ephesians 6:16 tells us to make good
use of our time, because the days are evil: In other
words, don't be a loafer or slothful.

Housework—a Team Effort

Because of the multiple responsibilities involved in
being a total homemaker, there should be a house-
work-sharing arrangement. Naturally, the number of
children in the family and the size of the home will
make a difference in the demands on the mother.
Each family must determine the amount of work required for comfortable living and then work together
as a team to accomplish it.

As each child has a birthday, assign him one more
responsibility that is his alone (empty wastebaskets,
make his own bed, dust and/or vacuum one room, fill
and/or empty the dishwasher, water plants, scour
sinks and bathtub, mow the lawn, and so forth). There
are advantages to having several children: Many hands
make light work!

One of the key factors in management is to check
up on those who work for you. In the home, the
mother—as the home manager—must be a "checker-
upper." In doing this, she is also training the child to

be dependable and to do a job well. The mother will need to organize herself, before she can expect to organize her family.

The children are on the team. What about the husband? Some will say that he is the provider and not expected to help around the house. It is this kind of thinking that has made women martyrs and open targets for the feminist movement. Everyone who lives in the home and helps to clutter it should participate on the team that cleans it up. There are numerous ways a husband can lighten the load for his wife. I know of husbands who insist on loading the dishwasher after every evening meal. Others feel the least they can do is vacuum the whole house once a week. Another brave father has arranged to give the three children their baths each night, dress them for bed, and finish with a good-night story and prayers.

The amount the husband is involved probably depends on the wife's obligations outside the home. If she is home all day, but wastes her time, she cannot expect her husband to come home from a day's work and do what she should have been doing earlier. However, if she has been busy mothering and homemaking during the day, there is little reason why her husband should not give her good assistance in the evening. The husband who comes home, goes promptly to his chair with the newspaper, moves only when dinner is called, and then returns immediately to his chair after the meal, to remain in a semiconscious state, can expect resentment and discord to grow in his home. This is not an example of a husband's love for his wife, but rather a selfish attitude that does not build a happy relationship.

Involvement Outside the Home

Though women are assigned to be the managers of the home, this does not necessarily sentence them to the home forever. A woman's responsibilities and priorities should be as follows: her relationship to God first, her husband second, and her children and home third. Any other involvements should follow her obligations at home. If she is able to keep these priorities in line and keep her attitude and spirit pleasing to God, she may be capable of including activities outside the home. When an extracurricular activity causes her to lose sight of her top priorities and affects her attitude, she is either not able or not ready to cope with other involvements. She should not allow anything to interfere with the basic priorities she was designed to fulfill. The responsibility of being the teacher to the children is clearly stated in Proverbs 1:8: "Hear, my son, your father's instruction, And do not forsake your mother's teaching," and again, in Proverbs 6:20, "My son, observe the commandment of your father, And do not forsake the teaching of your mother."

It is only fair to give consideration to the causes that conservative psychologist Urie Bronfenbrenner attributes to the problem with children and society.

Bronfenbrenner ascribed the alienation of the young and the rise of juvenile crime to the increase in divorce, working mothers, and the single-parent household. A mother's continual presence in the household during a child's growing up, Bronfenbrenner insisted, was essential. He deplored the increasing tendency of women to be employed away from home even if they had small children.[2]

You may not agree fully with this psychologist, but his concept is worthy of consideration. Children are only in the home for approximately sixteen to eighteen years, and those are the most important years of their lives. If a mother keeps her family priorities properly in line, everything she attempts will be in a position below that of her family.

When her children are of school age and a mother finds hours during the day when no one expects her to be home, rather than sitting at home bored, she should involve herself in an outside activity that challenges her and gives her a further sense of fulfillment. There are numerous opportunities awaiting her, depending on her interests and talents. Her church may offer her a field of women's ministries; her city may need volunteer hospital workers; her country may offer her a challenge in the moral/political world.

One neighbor of mine married young, had two babies rather close together, and did a great job of staying home and creating an atmosphere of love and learning for them. Finally the day came when both children were in school, and my friend felt a new freedom and a desire for additional challenge. Because she had married so young, she really had not had the time or opportunity to discover her gifts and interests. So she enrolled in an adult art class near her home, partly for convenience and partly because of a moderate enthusiasm in the subject. It was not long before it became very evident that she had ability that needed to be trained and encouraged. Today my neighbor has blossomed into a very fine artist of increasing renown. When she presents a show of her oil paintings, there are two children and a husband who stand by with great pride. They are proud of a mother who fulfilled her top three priorities with enthusiasm, and they are thankful that God has permitted her to branch out into a whole new dimension. She handles it well!

Some women may feel the pressure of high inflation and desire to help with family finances by seeking employment. If there is a need to brush up on certain skills, classes are available for most technical and nontechnical opportunities. It is highly possible for a woman to discover hidden talents at a time like this.

One of the dangers of branching out beyond the home is the tendency to accept the challenge of the business world, giving it a higher priority than it rightfully deserves. In doing so, something else must suffer. A woman's children, home, husband, or even God may be superseded by her new career. Priority is not determined solely by the amount of time spent on an activity, but rather by what would be given up, if need be, to keep the priorities in proper order.

Child-Care Problems

If it is necessary to use a baby-sitter or child-care center, the philosophy of either should be in agreement with what the child is taught in the home. Beliefs should be closely scrutinized in areas such as God, discipline, truthfulness, morals, authority, clean language, consistency of promises, standards of obedience, and so forth. This idea is not as farfetched as it may seem. I have had young mothers come to me, with great concern, because their two- and three-year-olds picked up four-letter words from the child-care center where they were enrolled. They will eventually hear these words in school and maybe even try them out, but a school that agrees with you on these issues is preferable to one where the teacher has no conscience about them. The teacher should reinforce your training and cooperate with you.

The leaders of the women's-rights movement are faithfully campaigning for government supported and controlled child-care centers. These would be staffed by professionals approved by the secular, humanist, educational system—who would omit God, morality, discipline, and many of the other things that a Christian parent would expect her child to be taught. Instead of getting this kind of anti-God, antimoral education at five or six, children would be getting it at the preschool ages of two, three, or four. The liberation leaders claim this is an ideal way to free mothers, so they can develop their own careers. This selfish motivation takes its toll at the expense of the children. What good is it to develop a productive career, if the responsibility to "train up a child in the way he should go" is not fulfilled? The finest executive position in the country cannot repair the heartbreak resulting from this kind of failure.

Child psychologist Selma Fraiberg has written a book on day-care centers, *Every Child's Birthright: In Defense of Mothering,* and declares they are not healthy places for small children to spend much time. In discussing this book, Solveig Eggerz comments:

> The child who spends most of his waking day in an environment of indifference is a likely candidate for what Fraiberg calls the disease of non-attachment, which is frequently incurable. These children grow into the "hollow men" of society, persons who, in their most harmful form, wander lonely and indifferent through life, and in the worst instances may be capable of blood-curdling crimes without a prick of conscience. Once a child is several years old, the chances of reversing this development are slim.[3]

Lee Salk, an authority on child development, believes that those couples who prefer to place their children in day-care centers, rather than taking care of them, should not have any children.[4]

However, if it is necessary to use the services of a baby-sitter or child-care center, be selective concerning who is helping to raise your children. Mothers should search for mother substitutes who can develop the personal attachment that a young child needs. There are many very fine church-sponsored child-care centers, which may be more in line with your beliefs and desires for your children. Be sure that whoever cares for your children can satisfactorily answer the questions that are important for the proper training and development of your precious possessions.

"The Cottage Industry"

Over the last three hundred years, our society has been through great changes. Where once the fields were crowded with masses of working farmers, they are now nearly empty. Crowded urban factories and offices have taken their place as the source of family income. Alvin Toffler states:

> Today it takes an act of courage to suggest that our biggest factories and office towers may, within our lifetimes, stand half empty, reduced to use as ghostly warehouses or converted into living space. Yet this is precisely what the new mode of production makes possible; a return to cottage industry on

a new, higher, electronic basis, and with it a new emphasis on the home as the center of society.[5]

Peter Tattle, Vice-President of Ortho Pharmaceutical Ltd. (Canada), says, "Fully seventy-five percent could work at home if we provided the necessary communications technology."[6]

Imagine a large number of mothers, able to stay at home and dedicate a part of their day to employment and financial assistance. Even though this technology is not ready for full-scale operation as yet, there are many women who are involved in a cottage-industry type of business. They have been successful in seeking out different types of work they can do at home on the kitchen table. This is beginning to be a respectable service to the business community and an important asset to the families of our nation.

Summary of Fulfillment or Frustration

A contented emotional response is not determined by whether or not the homemaker leaves the home to develop a career. If this were the case, there would not be so many discontented, gainfully employed mothers feeling guilt and frustration. On the other hand, there are numerous women at home who never leave "to seek their fortune," yet they are equally frustrated and upset.

It is not the career; it is not the home; it is the attitude of the heart and the response to God's command,

"In everything give thanks; for this is God's will for you in Christ Jesus" (1 Thessalonians 5:18). This is the heart attitude that produces a better self-image and responsiveness to God's will, develops a warmer relationship between a woman and her husband, enables her to establish a home atmosphere of love and learning for the children, and even allows her to accomplish outside achievements that reach beyond her greatest expectations.

9
Designed for Parenting

If a woman is designed to give life, it seems rather redundant to mention that she is to assist in parenting that child for the first several years of his life. Even though this was discussed as it pertained to home-making, there is much more that can and should be said about God's plan for raising and training children.

Just as God designed women to bring life into the world, He equipped them for nursing and caring for the children, to give them the proper beginning in life. Since the mother is the one who is intended to nurture and care for the needs of the children, she cannot and should not be expected to be the provider, as well.

In a recent issue of *Time* magazine, the validity of motherhood and the subject of the God-given maternal instinct were declared notions that have been out of fashion since the rise of feminism. However, scientists have confirmed that the crying of an infant affects the mother by stimulating the secretion of the hormone oxytocin, which causes erection of the nipples for nursing. The French feminist Elizabeth Badinter comments that even if maternal instinct is real, it can be overcome by removing the baby from the mother in the first few days after birth; then the motherly interest declines sharply. This is a defiant attempt to change the design that God had for motherhood, and will result in depriving both mother and child of the relationship and benefits that God intended should result from proper parenting.

There is no substitute for good mothering during a child's infancy, or for good mothering and good fathering later on.[1] When Proverbs includes both the mother and father in referring to the instruction and training of the children, it is not by happenstance. This is God's ideal for developing and preparing future generations.

Art of Parenting

There are many fine guidebooks that give instruction on the how-to of parenting. Dr. James Dobson is at the top of the list, with his books *Dare to Discipline, Hide or Seek,* and most recently, *The Strong-Willed Child.* At the risk of sounding immodest, let me suggest my own book *How to Develop Your Child's Temperament.*

There are, however, certain moral dangers of which a parent must be aware. It is crucial, for the happy outcome of the child's early development, that parents and other adults (teachers, relatives, and so forth) recognize the constitutional uniqueness of the child (particularly those quailties which are typically male or female), and not try to force him into being a type of person contrary to his basic nature. One aspect of the art of parenthood is the ability to recognize qualities in a child's personality and adapt to them in a way that leads to a harmonious interaction between parent and child.[2]

In other words, recognize and accept the child's sex immediately, planning his training and your relationship with him in a way that will build the qualities of the sex that God designed him to have. Of all the characteristics that deserve the most emphasis and clearest understanding by parents, the traits of the male and female are the most important. When the parents' influence and training are not in harmony with the basic characteristics of the child's sex, great harm, with far-reaching consequences, may result.

Allow little boys to be little boys and little girls to be little girls. Educators are influencing this area by blending the roles of male and female, so there is no distinction. Some teachers in the early grades are introducing games and activities that blur the sex differences, rather than clearly identifying them. The feminist influence has even reached school textbooks. Father is pictured doing household chores and nursing a sick child. Mother may be pictured climbing a telephone pole or working at the office, while father is doing the laundry. Textbook language is being changed to remove such words as *man, woman, mother, father, boy,* or *girl,* and replace them with nonsexist language.

The unisex movement and aspects of the women's liberation movement contribute to this blurring. The trend is to erase sex differences, not to accentuate

them. These social trends run counter to natural law: God designed male and female as distinct and different. The environment—parents, in particular— should evoke and reinforce these differences, not blur them, or worse, attempt to reverse them.[3]
    Dr. Rhoda L. Lorand, a respected clinical psychologist, commented on the danger of blurring the sexes.

Putting pressure on boys and girls to behave like the opposite sex is placing them under a great strain because these pressures are at odds with biological endowment. Therapists have begun to note the confusion and unhappiness resulting from the blurring of gender-identity. Conflicting pressures between environmental and instinctual drives hinder the development of a firm sense of identity as a male or female (an intended goal of Women's Lib), lacking which the individual cannot acquire stability, self-esteem, or clear-cut goals.

Moreover, it is taking all the joy and excitement out of life. Girls are made to feel ashamed of their longings to be courted and cherished, to be sexually attractive, to look forward to marriage, motherhood, and homemaking. Boys are made to feel ashamed of their chivalrous impulses. Feelings of protectiveness toward a girl and of manliness cause them to feel guilty and foolish, resulting in a retreat into passivity, while the girls end up unhappily trying to be sexual buddies of the boys. This unisex drive had its beginnings in the hippie movement and has been greatly intensified by all the publicity given by the communications media to the demands and accusations of the feminists (who really should be called masculinists, since they despise everything feminine).[4]

It is very dangerous to treat a little boy or little girl as a member of the opposite sex. When a little boy starts acting like a girl, the fault is in the rearing of the child, not in his genes. Advances should be made to correct the problem, and positive steps of change should be taken immediately. The sensitive parent will be aware of these tendencies, so they can be corrected at an early age, before the child reaches maturity. Involve little boys with father's companionship and little girls with mother's. Dad and son can go to the ball game or work on the car. Mother and daughter can work together to develop skills in sewing and cooking. This type of interrelationship must be worked on; it does not just happen. The woman was designed to lead the way in early training, because she is intended to be with the child more hours than the father. Therefore, the father must find time and ways to relate to his sons. She has been fashioned to sense a direct responsibility for the feelings and whereabouts of her child.

Parental Authority Over Child

A child who learns to yield to the loving leadership of his parents will one day submit to the other forms of authority with which he will be confronted later in life. Lack of respect for leadership produces rebellion and confusion. But most important, the child who yields to the loving authority of his parents will learn to yield to the loving leadership of his heavenly Father.

Child advocates are harming the lives of youth today by trying to remove them from parental authority. Children are caught in a tug-of-war between government control and parental authority. Richard Farson, author of *Birthrights: A Bill of Rights for Children,* is a strong supporter of child advocacy. These new supporters of children's rights are calling for civil rights for children and arguing that children will be helped most, not by protecting them, but by protecting their rights. He equates the protection of our children with enslavement. Child advocates claim that they, not parents, know what is best for children, just as protectionists of the past knew what was best for women and slaves. Common sense says that twentieth-century parents are not to their children what nineteenth-century planters were to their slaves.

Eliminate Child Spankings?

Farson also advocates that corporal punishment (spankings) should be eliminated. He accuses parents of using this "bodily violence" to force the child to submit to adult authority. He fails to use any terms regarding obedience to parents or punishment for acts of rebellion against authority.

In direct contrast to this dangerous philosophy is Ephesians 6:1–3: "Children, obey your parents in the Lord, for this is right. Honor your father and mother (which is the first commandment with a promise), That it may be well with you, and that you may live long on the earth."

The Swedish parliament decreed that after July 1, 1979, it became illegal for parents to spank or slap their children. Not only was any type of physical punishment outlawed, but parents were also forbidden to subject their children to "humiliating treatment." Included among this latter provision was parental refusal to talk to a child, depriving him of a meal, or reading his mail.

Swedish bureaucrats are churning out videotapes for school children, to advise them of their "constitutional rights," while the Swedish Red Cross is hiring an ombudsman to investigate children's complaints.[5] Only time will reveal what harm this will cause Swedish children who, like all children, need to be taught discipline and obedience for development and proper maturing.

God's Instruction for Discipline

The Bible has much to say about discipline and gives sufficient instruction on how to discipline a child. It always refers to a rod, when it speaks of correcting children. A few of the verses that give definite direction for disciplining a child are listed below:

He who spares his rod hates his son, But he who loves him disciplines him diligently.

Proverbs 13:24

Foolishness is bound up in the heart of a child; The rod of discipline will remove it far from him.

Proverbs 22:15

Do not hold back discipline from the child, Although you beat him [teach him] with the rod, he will not die.

Proverbs 23:13

The rod and reproof give wisdom, But a child who gets his own way brings shame to his mother.

Proverbs 29:15

A vital part of the art of parenting is the wisdom and knowledge of godly discipline, which requires teaching obedience to a higher authority. The only specific instruction given to children in the Bible relates to obedience to parents. Obedience is taught by proper discipline. The example has been set for parents by the heavenly Father, in Hebrews:

For those whom the Lord loves He disciplines, and He scourges every son whom He receives. It is for discipline that you endure; God deals with you as with sons; for what son is there whom his father does not discipline? But if you are without discipline, of which all have become partakers, then you

are illegitimate children and not sons. Furthermore, we had earthly fathers to discipline us, and
we respected them; shall we not much rather be
subject to the Father of spirits, and live?

Hebrews 12:6–9

The parent who does not assume the responsibility
of disciplining his child is treating the child as though
he were illegitimate. An undisciplined child will feel as
though he does not belong to anyone, and his self-esteem will be adversely affected.

True love for children requires proper discipline for
healthy development. The parent develops the attitude of discipleship in the child. A disciple is one who
obediently follows the teaching of his leader. It is this
same attitude that the Christian parent would desire
his child to transfer to the heavenly Father.

10
Who Is Truly Single?

The word *single* is such a broad term, in this twentieth century, yet it really does not tell much about the individual. One is called single if he or she is unmarried, either by choice or not. This person may be living at home with parents, or may be separated from and completely independent of family, or may have a cohabitation relationship (living together as husband and wife without marriage). Singleness can result from divorce or from the death of a partner, in which case, the single person may be left a parent or may have no dependents at all. Another form of single life that has come out of the closet in recent years is that of the homosexual, who may have a temporary attachment to someone of the same sex or a roaming interest in any number of people of the same gender. The more liberated our society becomes, the more the term *single* develops a loose meaning.

It is indeed unfortunate that the widowed Christian woman who has experienced a good marriage is today known as single. This puts her in the same category as the lesbian who has chosen a life-style of promiscuity and immorality. Dropping the term *widowed* for the more general term *single* adds dignity and acceptance to the homosexual life-style. This is just another subtle way of blending the gay community into the normal, accepted life-style of our society.

When speaking of a single person, I classify the type of singleness, using God's standards, so there is no misunderstanding of right and wrong.

Single virgin. A single virgin is one who has never married, by God's standards or society's, and has kept her body pure and holy.

Libertine single. This person does not hold a legal marriage contract, and by God's standards has broken the model of virginity (may also be a parent).

Cohabitation single. One who lives with a member of the opposite sex as husband and wife, without the bonds of legal marriage (may also be a parent).

Widowed single. The widow has been married, by the standards of both God and society, but has been separated from her partner by death, leaving her a widowed woman (may also be a parent).

Divorced single. She has also been legally married, but because of personal conflicts, society's marriage contract has been terminated (may also be a parent).

Lesbian single. The lesbian must be considered totally separate from other singles, since this is a distinctly different life-style, involving relations with members of the same sex, and is not recognized by God (1 Corinthians 6:9, 10) or society as an accepted marriage unit, though every attempt is being made by the feminists to have homosexuality included among approved family life-styles.

God's Standard for Singleness

Our very lives are a gift from God. Just as He has given us life, He also has a plan for how we live that life. God, who knows the end from the beginning, also knows what is best for us and how we should live. In today's society, there is a trend to associate more prestige with the single life than with marriage. However, God's Word places greater emphasis on marriage and family relationships. We have become victimized by society, rather than followers of God's choices. God has selected three life-styles for women: single virginity, married, or widowed. Any other styles of living become human choices, not God's. The libertines, cohabitants, divorced, and lesbians are results of selfish influences, not the options God has for His children.

Even though God does not approve of these lifestyles, this does not mean such a person is forever beyond His love and forgiveness. Quite the contrary. God, in His great mercy, will forgive and justify the lesbian, libertine, cohabitant, and divorced, just as He said in 1 Corinthians 6:9–11:

Or do you not know that the unrighteous shall not inherit the kingdom of God? Do not be deceived; neither fornicators [libertines, cohabitants], nor idolators, nor adulterers [most common cause for divorce], nor effeminate, nor homosexuals [lesbians], nor thieves, nor the covetous, nor drunkards [cause for divorce also], nor revilers, nor swindlers, shall inherit the kingdom of God. And such were some of you; but you were washed, but you were sanctified, but you were justified in the name of the Lord Jesus Christ, and in the Spirit of our God.

It is possible for the lesbian to see the immorality of her life-style and confess it to Christ as sin. When that confession is genuine and motivated by a sincere heart, God has promised forgiveness. She will be forgiven, cleansed, sanctified, and justified in the name of the Lord Jesus Christ.

I have seen the reality of forgiveness in the lives of several who came to the realization that their life-style was not God's will for them, but rather a result of their own selfish, immoral choices. One by one, I have watched forgiveness start a transformation in their lives. However, this first requires a recognition of their life-style as sinful, and secondly, a sincere desire for change. The standard excuse, "Once a homosexual, always a homosexual," is a myth. I have seen too many come out of that style of living to believe that it cannot be done, and some after years of intimate involvement with members of the same sex.

The same can be said for the libertine life-style, or the cohabitant, or the adulterer. God's forgiveness knows no limitations. It is the individual who limits what God can do in his life. Remember that God is "not wishing for any to perish but for all to come to repentance" (2 Peter 3:9).

Beware of Heart Problems

There is a certain stigma placed on the truly single woman today. She is generally considered lonely, miserable, in search of companionship, and, to put it bluntly, "on the look." And, of course, there are some men who consider themselves the answer to a single woman's prayer, without offering any commitment. It is not uncommon for a man to consider "consoling" several lonely women at the same time. If the single person is seeking companionship, these acts of kindness may be misunderstood. When she learns that the friendship does not include commitment, the realization may plunge her into depression and sometimes even despair.

Just recently I had a long counseling session with a single woman who is over thirty. Her self-image was not too strong, to begin with, and as her story unfolded, I could anticipate the anguish she was suffering. She had never received much attention from members of the opposite sex, yet she wanted to be married and be able to establish a home and family. So when an older gentleman began to show some interest, inviting her to dinner on several occasions, taking her to concerts and musicals, on bike trips, and even holding intimate dinners in his lovely home, she began to assume it was more than mere acts of kindness and expected a reasonable commitment from him. He, however, would make no promises and did not even care to discuss the relationship. Soon she began to see that she was headed down a dead-end street that promised no future. Unfortunately, her heart and emotions were already involved, to the point of being willing to make a lifetime marriage agreement. It would be impossible to express the pain she has suffered and the harm that has been done to her self-image. She has retreated within herself, in an attempt to gain control of her feelings. Only the grace of God can restore her heart and emotions to normalcy.

Feminist Labels

Single women are more readily labeled as feminists than married women, because of the more liberal lifestyles available to them. The feminist leaders are strong supporters of homosexual rights, amoral libertine conduct, and men and women living together without marriage. Married women are expected to be committed to their husbands, thus eliminating the vast majority of them from the amoral feminist philosophy. This does not mean that most singles are feminists. Absolutely not. There are countless morally minded single women who maintain the personal philosophy of heterosexual commitment. Because of circumstances in life beyond their control, they are unable at present to practice that belief, yet they hold that sacred teaching as a vital part of their life's philosophy.

Blessings of the Single Life

Not every single woman is lonely, miserable, or seeking permanent companionship. There are many who have found contentment in the single life, which is essentially a matter of accepting God's will each day, one day at a time. God's specific will today may be different than His will next year. The important factor is for a woman to accept what may not be her choice but is God's choice for her today.

Somewhere along the road, a single lady must face the possibility that God never intended her to marry or to remarry and that she may have been selected to live without the benefit of marriage for the rest of her life. Since there are 109 women to every 100 men, it stands to reason that some women will not be able to marry. There is great consolation available in the Scripture, which places the single woman in a special relationship to God. "And the woman who is unmarried, and the virgin, is concerned about the things of the Lord, that she may be holy both in body and spirit; but one who is married is concerned about the things of the world, how she may please her husband" (1 Corinthians 7:34).

This special relationship between the single woman and God is forever. Remember, if God calls you to a single life, He wants you to have a beautiful relationship with Himself, keeping yourself holy in body and spirit.

11
Women–the Endangered Species

Most women have been brought up under the accepted philosophy that women are a unique yet distinct part of society. There are, admittedly, certain problems that need to be dealt with and resolved, but the same is true in many areas of our culture. Laws have been and are continually being made that will correct these wrongs. We are by no means a perfect nation. Generally speaking, however, womanhood has been revered, respected, and held in a position of distinction to a higher degree here than in any other country in the world.

One need only travel in foreign countries to see that women have been exalted in nations where Christianity has been allowed to flourish and abound. Yet in countries embracing an anti-God philosophy, women have experienced suppression and inferior, nondistinctive treatment.

Just a few years ago, my husband and I traveled throughout many countries of the world. We were able to observe firsthand the direct correlation between a country's treatment of its women and the religion of that country. The more heathen the country, the less humane was the treatment of women. In anti-God, socialist countries, where all are said to be equal, there was no respect or distinction for womanhood. After traveling in five of these socialist countries and observing the equality of the people, it became readily apparent that women are much better off in America, where (until recently) femininity has been honored, as God designed it to be.

Probably the most painful sight I can recall occurred in one of the largest socialist countries. I watched two women, both past sixty years of age, just outside the Kremlin wall in Moscow. One was standing on top of huge chunks of broken cement in the back of a dump truck, while the other little lady stood on the ground, lifting and handing the forty- to fifty-pound pieces of cement to the lady in the truck. The truck was almost full, but there was still much more to load. At that age, they were probably grandmothers, however, without the benefits and esteem usually associated with the position. My mind raced quickly to the ladies in my church and community who were close to the same age, and I was aware of the respect and dignity usually given to them. Christianity exalts womanhood, while supporters of an anti-God philosophy want to equalize male and female positions.

Many of the leaders of the feminist movement in America are strong advocates of a socialistic society. A quick cure for that mentality would be to spend a year in a socialist country as an average female citizen. The strategy to revolutionize the American society into a socialistic, humanistic nation holds women as the number-one target. Betty Friedan, commonly referred to as the mother of the feminist movement, claimed in a recent interview that the women's-rights movement is structured for two phases. The first phase involves changing the role of women by the passage of the Equal Rights Amendment. This is scheduled to be the "unshackling" of women from the traditional family structure and the loss of distinctive female characteristics. The second phase is bent on changing every institution in our society to agree with the philosophy of the feminists, including the institutions of marriage, the family, education, the military, religion, and so forth.

Personal Conviction

Some women have wondered why I have taken such a definite stand opposing the women's-rights movement. My emphasis in speaking and writing has always been on helping women and strengthening families. Therefore, why am I against a movement that appears to be directed toward the improvement of the role of women in society?

Upon studying the history of the feminist movement, it is evident that the demands of women's-rights advocates are not new, but simply a repeat of history.

Perhaps one of the best sources for the history of the feminist movement is Lawrence Lader. As an abortion pioneer, he was a friend of Margaret Sanger (founder of Planned Parenthood) as well as of Betty Friedan (founder of the National Organization for Women). In his book, so aptly titled *Abortion II: Making the Revolution,* Lader describes the merging of the abortion movement and the feminist movement into one, which thereby kicked off the "revolution."

> The publication of Friedan's *Feminine Mystique* in 1963, and the founding of the National Organization for Women in 1966 (these two events) marked the dividing line between the old feminism of rights and the new feminism of liberation—Friedan and Neofeminism erupted on a wave of technology. For it was the technology of contraception, the birth-control pill, that made possible the radicalization of women.[1]

It is this philosophy that causes me to oppose the ERA, because the amendment is only a portion of the total goal of the feminist movement. The ERA is just a stepping-stone to the ultimate goal of revolution in our existing American society: a change to an atheistic, humanist nation. The passage of the amendment is only one cog in the wheel. If not by means of the ERA, they will strive to accomplish their goals through some other method.

The Feminist Dream

The American woman has been flooded with ERA promises and arguments. The simple fifty-two words of the amendment have been applied, like healing salve, to cure the "unequal" treatment of women in this country. Unfortunately, it is becoming evident that the side effects of this medication are more serious than the disease itself. It is the feminist dream that all wrongs will be righted with the passage of this amendment. The wording of the Equal Rights Amendment is as follows:

Section 1. Equality of rights under the law shall not be denied or abridged by the United States or by any State on account of sex.

Section 2. The Congress shall have the power to enforce by appropriate legislation the provisions of this article.

Section 3. This amendment shall take effect two years after the date of ratification.

"Equality of rights" is the magic phrase. We are all in favor of basic equal rights, but to add an amendment to the Constitution of the United States, whereby equal rights must be tested in the courts and enforced by federal law, demands close scrutiny by every concerned individual.

As I travel around the country, I often ask ERA supporters why they favor its ratification. Almost invariably, their answer involves equal pay for equal work, equal job-promotion opportunities, or equal treatment in hiring, and so forth. If this is what is expected of the ERA, there is no need for it. There is already legislation in operation that deals with such forms of discrimination between the sexes.

> Equal pay for equal work is covered by:
> Civil Rights Act of 1964
> Equal Pay Act of 1963
> Equal Employment Opportunity Act of 1972
> Equal treatment is covered by:
> Fourteenth Amendment
> Higher Education Act of 1972
> Comprehensive Health Manpower Training Act of 1971
> Nurse Training Act of 1971
> Comprehensive Employment and Training Act of 1973
> Federal Equal Credit Opportunity Act of 1975[2]

Because of these existing laws, millions of dollars have been received by women whose cases against large corporations in our country were brought to court. Some complain that even though we have these laws, there are still inequities and discrimination. If the laws are not being properly enforced, the solution is to strengthen and expand the services that implement the laws already in existence, not create new laws that make enforcement an even greater problem.

The passage of the ERA would not eliminate economic and social injustices. The legal process we now have would still be necessary, to correct illegal actions.

Far too many sincere people have been led to believe that the ERA is the "miracle drug" which will wipe out all of our nation's discrimination "ills." Professor Paul A. Freund of Harvard Law School, one of the foremost legal scholars in the country, points out that it is far better to have "specific pills for specific ills" than simply one "broad-spectrum drug" designed for every ill, and which carries with it "unwanted and uncertain side effects."[3] We need to enforce what we already have, not pass more legislation.

More Federal Control

Section 2 of the amendment guarantees more federal involvement in private lives and deprives the individual states of rights they previously held. The ERA would require federal legislation in any field in which there is now any differential treatment of the sexes. Most of these are now in the hands of individual states and communities:

Marriage and the Family
Divorce and Alimony

> Child Care and Custody
> Adoptions
> Inheritance Laws
> Abortion Laws
> Public Accommodations and Facilities
>   Hospitals
>   Prisons
>   Public Buildings
>   Schools
> Armed Forces
> Labor Laws
> Insurance Rates and Regulations
> Laws about Homosexuality[4]

The passage of the ERA would greatly increase the power of the federal government. As it stands currently, any state law that does not deal fairly with women can be repealed by the state legislature, which is controlled by the voters. Because of Section 2, all state laws involving the sexes would be null and void.

What Will the ERA Accomplish?

The amendment *will* prevent us from making reasonable differentiations between men and women, based on the actual differences of childbearing and physical strength. ERA *will* force upon us the rigid, unisex, gender-free mandate demanded by the women's-liberation movement, and *will* transfer the power to apply this mandate to the federal government and the federal courts.[5]

ERA will require state and federal laws to be "neuterized," removing "sexist" words such as man, woman, male, female, husband, and wife. Neutral words are already the norm in some areas, but in others, a definite change will be required. One important change would be in the military. The Selective Service Act would be revised to read "all persons" must register for the draft, instead of "all male citizens." Congress would lose the right to exempt women from the draft. That exemption, based on sex, would be discrimination, and therefore unconstitutional. The same is true for exempting women from combat duty.[6]

Prior to the passage of the ERA in the Senate, Senator Ervin proposed two amendments to protect women: number 1065 would have exempted women from compulsory military training, and number 1066 would have exempted women from combat. Both proposals were rejected. This refusal to attach these two restrictions to the ERA is proof of the true intent of the supporters of the amendment.

The amendment will nullify any state law that now makes it illegal to marry another of the same sex. To deny a marriage license to any person because of sex would be unconstitutional.[7] This is a back-door attempt to legalize homosexuality. Marriage would grant homosexual couples the legal right to adopt children and to blend into society as an accepted family unit.

The ERA is essentially a prohibition—one that allows no distinctions between men and women, boys and girls, no matter how reasonable or necessary these distinctions may have seemed in the past. In short, this amendment seeks to outlaw all sexual discrimination by outlawing all sexual distinctions.[8]

It is not beyond expectation that the passage of this amendment would be interpreted as a stamp of approval by the people of the United States on the Supreme Court's 1973 decision on abortion. Since abortions are required by one sex only, any law prohibiting them would be "sexist" legislation and therefore unconstitutional.

Do We Oppose Change?

Change is acceptable and desirable, as long as it does not interfere with or modify God's standards for men and women, boys and girls.

The secular humanists are in favor of blind change, believing everything is in a state of change and moving upward. They have no stablizing law by which to determine the value of change.

When considering any alteration in laws and lifestyles, weighing the changes in light of biblical principles should always be first and foremost. Will these changes help people live in obedience to God's laws? If not, we must be opposed to any change that will interfere with or interrupt God's standards for male and female.

12
Conflicting Philosophies

Why is there such growing conflict over the traditional values and morals of our country? Why are these God-given beliefs being tested and tried, and why are many failing, with governmental approval? There appears to be an undermining of all truths that Christians hold: the belief in God, as the Creator of all things; definite distinctions between male and female; life beginning at conception; God's institution of the family; homosexuality as a sin; definite standards of morality and immorality.

The answer is profoundly revealed in my husband's book *The Battle for the Mind.* I encourage you to read it. Put simply, the answer is that America is involved in a battle between two philosophies: the wisdom of man (humanism) versus the wisdom of God (biblical revelation).

Man's Wisdom

Humanism is a man-centered philosophy that attempts to solve the problems of man and the world independently of God.

The wisdom of man, often called secular humanism today, can be traced back to the rudimentary writings of man. In fact, only two lines of reasoning permeate all of literature: biblical revelation (the wisdom of God) and the wisdom of man. All books are based either on man's thoughts or God's thoughts.[1]

When a person begins to grasp this concept, it becomes apparent why we are in conflict today over the value of human life, independent sex roles, the origin of man, immorality, and the structure and value of the family. A decision made independently of God's wisdom is totally different from one based on truth from God's Word.

The philosophy of humanism is set forth in the *Humanist Manifesto*. The *Humanist Manifesto I* was completed in 1933, by a group of thirty-four liberal humanists in the United States. Forty years later, in 1973, the *Humanist Manifesto II* was drafted as a more extensive and comprehensive update of the previous document.

God's Wisdom

The wisdom of God is found in the pages of the Holy Bible, from the thirty-nine books of the Old Testament through the twenty-seven books of the New Testament. The earliest manuscripts, which date back to the fourth century, are still in existence, and hundreds of manuscripts and translations of both the Old and New Testaments have been written since then. "The same God that divinely inspired men to write His Matchless Word has divinely preserved it through the centuries, so that we may say with the Lord Himself, 'Thy Word is Truth!' "[2]

"Knowledgeable humanists look upon the church and its doctrinal absolutes as the greatest enemy of mankind. More than an enemy, the church is a threat to humanism, for its leaders recognize that the only group that can save the Western world from the humanistic mind control of the Communist countries is the church."[3] That is the source of the growing conflict in our American society.

Betty Friedan, founder of the National Organization for Women (N.O.W.) and renowned "mother of the feminist movement," is one of the signers of the *Humanist Manifesto II*. It is this philosophy, which she endorses and which is revealed in the *Humanist Manifestos*, that permeates the beliefs of the feminist movement. This is why Christian women *must* oppose the feminist movement and the Equal Rights Amendment. The amendment is simply legalizing the means for imposing the philosophy of humanism on American society. Feminist leaders have boldly stated that our American culture is in the midst of a great societal change. That change will include our morality, ethics, values, consciousness, education, and religion.

A close examination of just a few of the issues under fire by the humanists are listed on the following pages, with a comparison from the Word of God.

Creation

   Humanism: "Religious humanists regard the universe as self-existing and not created . . . that man is a part of nature and that he has emerged as the result of a continuous process."[4]

   God's Word: "For in Him all things were created, both in the heavens and on earth, visible and invisible, whether thrones or dominions or rulers or authorities—all things have been created through Him and for Him" (Colossians 1:16). "In the beginning God created the heavens and the earth" (Genesis 1:1).

Value of Human Life

   Humanism: "The right to birth control, abortion, and divorce should be recognized."[5] "To enhance freedom and dignity the individual must experience a full range of *civil liberties* in all societies. . . . It also includes a recognition of an individual's right to die with dignity, euthanasia, and the right to suicide."[6]

   God's Word: "You shall not murder" (Exodus 20:13).

Morality

   Humanism: "In the area of sexuality, we believe that intolerant attitudes, often cultivated by orthodox religions and puritanical cultures, unduly repress sexual conduct. . . . While we do not approve of exploitive, denigrating forms of sexual expression, neither do we wish to prohibit, by law or societal sanction, sexual behavior between consenting adults."[7]

God's Word: "Or do you not know that the unrighteous shall not inherit the kingdom of God? Do not be deceived; neither fornicators, nor idolators, nor adulterers, nor effeminate, nor homosexuals, nor thieves, nor the covetous, nor drunkards, nor revilers, nor swindlers, shall inherit the kingdom of God" (1 Corinthians 6:9, 10).

Existence of Supernatural God

Humanism: "We find insufficient evidence for belief in the existence of a supernatural; it is either meaningless or irrelevant to the question of the survival and fulfillment of the human race. As non-theists, we begin with humans not God, nature not deity."[8]

God's Word: "In the beginning was the Word, and the Word was with God, and the Word was God" (John 1:1).

Eternal Salvation

Humanism: "No deity will save us; we must save ourselves. . . . Promises of immortal salvation or fear of eternal damnation are both illusory and harmful."[9]

God's Word: "For God so loved the world, that He gave His only begotten Son, that whoever believes in Him should not perish, but have eternal life" (John 3:16). "For the wages of sin is death, but the free gift of God is eternal life in Christ Jesus our Lord" (Romans 6:23).

The *Humanist Manifestos I and II* should be called the bible of the religion of humanism. It is a religion by their own admission. Just as the Bible states the beliefs, morals, and standards of living for the Christian, so the *Humanist Manifestos I and II* set forth humanism's beliefs, values, and goals.

Humanism is based on five basic tenets: atheism; evolution; amorality; autonomous, self-centered man; and a socialistic, one-world view.[10] In direct contrast, Christianity has five fundamental beliefs: God; Creation; morality; servants of God; and a compassionate world view.[11] The struggle intensifies, as the two philosophies work to influence and gain control of society. When the conflict involves atheism versus God, evolution versus Creation, amorality versus morality, self-centered man versus servants of God, and socialistic, one-world view versus compassionate world view, there is no neutral ground for agreement.

For instance, in considering the subject of abortion, the humanist—who makes his decisions totally independently of God, based on self-centered influence—has no guilty conscience in deciding that abortion involves the individual woman's control over her own body. The Christian takes several things into consideration: that God is the Creator of life, that we are here to be His servants, that God places a high premium on human life, and that God has instructed us not to murder. Therefore, abortions are not pleasing to God.

Every moral issue of our society, when weighed in the light of humanist belief versus God's teaching, will produce opposing conclusions of right and wrong.

Controlling Philosophy

American Christians are slowly waking up to the fact that the humanists have been gradually infiltrating the key areas of our society, in order to impose their philosophy on us. The areas of influence that humanists currently control are the fields of education, the media, organizations, and government itself. A complete, detailed explanation of humanist control in America is found in chapter 8 of *The Battle for the Mind*. Every Christian should read this book, particularly chapter 8, to be informed of the influence we have allowed humanists to have in our country.

However, it is not too late. There is a need for moral awakening in America. We need to recognize who our enemy really is: not other Christians, but the amoral humanists who have set about to destroy our God-given beliefs and morals. The humanists would like to intimidate the Christian with the accusation that he has a lack of intelligence and good reason.

Humanists still believe that traditional theism, especially faith in the prayer-hearing God, assumed to love and care for persons, to hear and understand their prayers, and to be able to do something about them, is an unproved and outmoded faith. Salvationism, based on mere affirmation, still appears as harmful, diverting people with false hopes of heaven hereafter. Reasonable minds look to other means for survival.[12]

Christians—Wake Up!

In other words, the humanist is saying that the faith (and even the mind) of anyone who believes in prayer, a God who answers prayer, or salvation and heaven, is unreasonable and outmoded. The millions of Christians whose prayers have been answered by a loving God should be jarred from their apathy and realize that humanism is the real enemy. Likewise, the millions who have experienced a personal faith in God by salvation and the blessed hope of heaven should be jolted by the threat of the humanists to alter and reconstruct religion to suit their philosophy.

We are told that there are only 275,000 humanists. The latest Gallup polls indicate 69 million believe in life after death. The humanists are in the minority, yet we have allowed them to occupy positions of leadership in our nation. Last, and most important, we have God on our side. But we cannot sit back, waiting for God to perform miracles. He works through men to accomplish His will.

We are in the midst of a moral crisis, and the conflict will increase until Christians wake up and rise up to defend the truth that is unchanging and unalterable!

13
Feminine Influence on Our Nation

In the past decade, there have been only a few isolated female defenders of morality and truth, with the majority of women preferring to remain comfortable and undisturbed by negative thoughts.

Probably the most influential and persistent has been Phyllis Schlafly, who has actively been defending our cause for many years. She is the founder and president of Eagle Forum, but more important than that is her success as a wife, mother, author, lawyer, and effective speaker. The Christian women of America can thank this great lady for holding back the floodwaters of the feminist movement and the ERA, while at the same time encouraging the rest of us to wake up and join the battle.

Phyllis Schlafly was one of the three people God used to help open my eyes to the dangers of the feminist movement and to encourage my involvement. Since that time, a few ill-informed people have asked if I am in competition with Phyllis or duplicating the efforts of her Eagle Forum. For the record, let me state that Phyllis Schlafly is a very gifted woman and has my highest respect; we have a great working relationship, she is a *dear* friend, and I am always in support of Eagle Forum. The conflict involving our nation leaves no room or time for anyone who is on an ego trip or trying to make a name for herself. It will take many of us, working side by side, to defend morality and truth and to protect the rights of our families. There is a need for many Phyllis Schlaflys and many Beverly La Hayes, to accomplish what needs to be done in America.

What Can I Do?

As I travel across the country speaking for Family Life Seminars and Concerned Women for America rallies, probably the question I am asked most often by women is, "What can I do?" Women are quick to respond, when they hear of more government control and intrusion into their homes and families, and they are eager to protect their children. When they learn what the philosophy of the feminist movement really is, they are ready to be involved.

This is not a day for women to be silent. Silence today is interpreted as agreement with feminism. When the feminist leaders stand up and tell the media that they are speaking for all American women, your silence will be an affirmation of that statement. It is this very experience that caused me to do something about it. When I heard one feminist speak on national

television and announce that she was speaking for the
women of our nation, I audibly responded, "You are
not speaking for me!" I decided making that statement
in my living room was fine, but it would have no influence on the nation. I needed to be saying that in my
community, state, and nation, if necessary. I guess my
question really was, "What can I do?"

In answering that question, let me stress the importance of aligning yourself with an existing organization that is standing against immorality and standing
for the traditional family. This is not only for your own
information; the strength of numbers is very important. A single voice crying out against immorality will
not be heard over the din and roar of the amoral humanists. There are many groups that deserve consideration; you need to find the one that will best suit
your interests and priorities. But, by all means, find
one. Lend your name and support, whether with time,
money, or both. When an organization steps into the
front of the battle, one of the first questions asked by
the media is, "How many members do you represent?" The organization that comes out with strength
of numbers is the one that will be heard. You may have
noticed that when N.O.W. is mentioned in the news, it
is often followed by a comment about its membership
of 100,000 to 110,000 women. The organization you
choose should be able to keep you informed on current
issues and instruct you on what you can do to speak
out against amorality.

Vote Morality

Every Christian man and woman has the responsibility to be a registered voter. The individual who does not exercise his right to have a voice in government is not obedient to Scripture. Not only are we to vote, but we should be informed voters and know how each candidate stands on morality. You can have an influence on our society by supporting those candidates running for public office who will vote for the family and morality.

Concerned Women for America

After reading my husband's book *The Battle for the Mind,* I realized that he had told the story of Concerned Women for America and how it began. Rather than repeat it, let me continue the story. This organization was formed to give women an answer to their question "What can I do?" It is designed for the Christian woman who is concerned about the feminist movement gaining control, the immoral condition of our country, and the increasing intrusion of government into the family. A monthly newsletter is sent to members (members are subscribers to the newsletter), at a minimal cost per year, to educate, inform, and motivate a unified action of opposition.

Prayer is such a vital part in resolving the conflicts between humanism and God's Word that CWA has also organized prayer chapters in every state of the nation.

(Additional information regarding the newsletter or prayer chapters can be obtained by writing Concerned Women for America, P.O. Box 20376, El Cajon, California 92021.) The chapters are open to anyone who believes in prayer and the fact that our God is a prayer-answering God. Monthly prayer alerts are sent to each member of a prayer chapter, with a focus on specific prayer requests. No extra meetings are required, as members pray individually at home. Contrary to what the *Humanist Manifesto* states about prayer, we have seen God answer many requests. Prayer is a reality. The irony is that prayer, which the humanists claim is outmoded and unproven, may be the very tool God will use to defeat their cause. "[If] My people who are called by My name humble themselves and pray, and seek My face and turn from their wicked ways, then I will hear from heaven, will forgive their sin, and will heal their land" (2 Chronicles 7:14).

Before we can expect God to move in our nation, we Christians must pray with humility, seek God, and turn from our wicked ways; then we can expect God to heal our land and restore truth in our country.

The growth of CWA has been an indication of the awakening concern of Christians across the nation. In the first year, over 94,000 women indicated their support and interest. Before the second year is over, membership may well exceed 150,000 women. When you consider the 69 million adults who have a personal faith in Jesus Christ, you realize that we are barely scratching the surface. There is much to be done, in stirring Christian women to action.

I envision thousands of Bible-believing churches one day establishing CWA prayer chapters within their women's groups, to pray for morality and a return to truth. It will take something of that magnitude to awaken and unify the Christian voice against the dangers of amoral humanism.

The Bible Commands Involvement

On many occasions we have heard Christians comment that the Bible warns of these evil days and that Christ is coming to remove us from the chaos and immorality, so why should we get so upset about the condition of our nation? It is true that Christ is returning for those who trust in Him, but He has also left us with warnings and instructions on our involvement in this world: "See to it that no one takes you captive through philosophy and empty deception, according to the tradition of men, according to the elementary principles of the world, rather than according to Christ" (Colossians 2:8).

We are warned that there will be a deceiving philosophy based on man's wisdom, not on Christ's, and that Christians are not to be taken in by it. What an appropriate verse for the day in which we live! Furthermore, we are told to expose those who are involved in evil deeds. "And do not participate in the unfruitful deeds of darkness, but instead even expose them" (Ephesians 5:11).

But that is not all. We would all agree that the teaching in Matthew 5:14 is ours to obey: "You are the light of the world." Christians have long been involved in seminars and special classes on sharing our faith more effectively. We have organized programs and efforts to allow our light to shine more brightly, but we have sadly neglected the verse immediately preceding that one: "You are the salt of the earth; but if the salt has become tasteless, how will it be made salty again? It is good for nothing any more, except to be thrown out and trampled under foot by men" (Matthew 5:13).

We are told to be salty and have a seasoning influence for righteousness in the world. If our influence (or saltiness) loses its effect, it is good for nothing. How many of us have attended a seminar or participated in a program to teach us how to be a more effective, salty Christian? Only in recent months has this become more widely accepted.

Salt is used for several different purposes that can be related to our influence on society. Salt has long been used as a preservative to prevent spoilage, particularly with meat. Our influence should be to preserve righteousness and truth. The substance of salt has had a healing effect for cuts and bleeding. Dentists have used saltwater wash as a treatment after minor mouth surgery. Our influence can have a healing effect on the sickness of our nation. The most common use of salt has been to influence the flavor of food. Anyone who has been on a salt-free diet can attest to the fact that food without salt is rather bland and tasteless. Salt enhances the flavor of food. The Christian who is the salt of the earth will influence society for righteousness and truth, and he should enhance the community around him. Permit me to go one step further. Salt makes a person thirsty. The salty Christian should also create a thirst for righteousness. When this thirst has been sufficiently aroused, the effects of being the light of the world should reap great rewards.

Unfortunately, the majority of Christian women have been "tasteless" citizens, having little influence on the righteousness of our nation. We have been quiet and uninvolved, while the feminists have been aggressively promoting amorality and humanism. It is time for Christian women in our nation to become aggressively salty in prayer and action, as we work together to restore moral standards and an acknowledgment of God's Word as truth in America.

Feminine Dedication

The Christian woman's motivation to be involved in moral restoration and preservation is a great deal different from the feminist motivation toward developing a libertine society. The feminist leader is dedicated to the humanistic philosophy; she is self-centered and committed to creating an amoral culture. When Betty

Friedan claims to have dedicated the rest of her life to changing America into a humanist society, she is exhibiting total commitment to the philosophy in which she believes. The Christian woman needs that kind of dedication and commitment to a philosophy that she knows is truth because it is based on God's Word. Furthermore, God has commanded her to be an influence for righteousness in our nation. She is motivated because of the effects on her children and her home. She must be dedicated to involvement in preserving morals and protecting her own femininity and her God-given rights as a woman. In doing this, she will also be preparing a moral tomorrow for her daughters, so they may be the women God designed them to be.

Designed to Wear an Armor

As has been previously stated, we object to women going into military combat. But there is one battle for which God's Word has prepared us:

> Finally, be strong in the Lord, and in the strength of His might. Put on the full armor of God, that you may be able to *stand firm against the schemes of the devil.* For our struggle is not against flesh and blood, but against the rulers, against the powers, against the world forces of this darkness, against the spiritual forces of wickedness in the heavenly places. Therefore, take up the full armor of God,

that you may be able to resist in the evil day, and having done everything, to stand firm.

Ephesians 6:10–13
italics mine

My prayer is that God will find us faithful in standing firm against the schemes of the devil. Will we be able to stand before Almighty God one day and say, "I did everything to stand firm against evil"?

I am convinced we could turn the tide against the humanist movement and its amoral influence, if every Christian woman would do what God has designed her to do: expose the evil deeds of darkness, since she is a salty influence for righteousness and truth. Then women can be free, indeed!

References

Chapter 1: Woman—Chance or Design?

1. *Humanist Manifestos I and II* (Buffalo, N.Y.: Prometheus Books, 1977), p. 8.

Chapter 2: Fashioned by God

1. *Ibid.*, p. 17.

Chapter 3: Designed to Give Life

1. Bernard N. Nathanson, M.D., with Richard N. Ostling, *Aborting America* (Garden City, N.Y.: Doubleday & Co., Inc., 1979), p. 250.
2. *Humanist Manifestos I and II*, pp. 18, 19.
3. Nathanson, pp. 26, 27.
4. Jean Staker Garton, *Who Broke the Baby?* (Minneapolis, MN: Bethany Fellowship, Inc., 1979), p. 30.
5. *The Human Life Review* (Vol. 1, No. 3, Summer 1975), p. 5.

Chapter 4: Subordinate, but Not Inferior

    1. David R. Nicholas, *What's a Woman to Do . . . in the Church?* (Scottsdale, AZ: Good Life Productions, Inc., 1979), pp. 28, 29.

    2. Beverly LaHaye, *The Spirit-Controlled Woman* (Irvine, CA: Harvest House Publishers, 1976), p. 71.

Chapter 5: Designed for Pleasure

    1. Letha Scanzoni, *Sex and the Single Eye* (Grand Rapids: Zondervan Publishing House, 1968), p. 31.

    2. James Dobson, *What Wives Wish Their Husbands Knew About Women* (Wheaton: Tyndale House Publishers, 1975), p. 114.

    3. Tim and Beverly LaHaye, *The Act of Marriage* (Grand Rapids: Zondervan Publishing House, 1976), p. 15.

Chapter 6: Is There a Place for Women in the Church?

    1. Letha Scanzoni and Nancy Hardesty, *All We're Meant to Be* (Waco, TX: Word Books, 1975), p. 171.

    2. William Barclay, *The Letter to the Romans* (Edinburgh: The Saint Andrews Press, 1958), pp. 231, 232.

Chapter 7: Distinctive in Being a Woman

1. Gene A. Getz, *The Measure of a Woman* (Glendale, CA: Regal Books, 1977), p. 76.

Chapter 8: The Modern Woman—Fulfilled or Frustrated as Homemaker?

1. Betty Friedan, *The Feminine Mystique* (New York: Dell Publishing Co., Inc., 1977), p. 238.
2. Carl N. Degler, *At Odds* (New York: Oxford University Press, 1980), p. 451.
3. Solveig Eggerz, "What Child Care Advocates Won't Tell You," *Human Events* (May 20, 1978), p. 13.
4. Harold Voth, M.D., *The Castrated Family* (Sheed, Andrews and McMeel, Inc., 1977), p. 8.
5. Alvin Toffler, *The Third Wave* (New York: William Morrow and Company, Inc., 1980), p. 210.
6. *Ibid.*, p. 213.

Chapter 9: Designed for Parenting

1. Voth, p. 9.
2. *Ibid.*, p. 14.
3. *Ibid.*, p. 16.
4. Phyllis Schlafly, *The Power of the Positive Woman* (New York: Arlington House Publishers, 1977), p. 216.
5. *San Diego Union,* May 20, 1979.

Chapter 11: Women—the Endangered Species

1. Lawrence Lader, *Abortion II: Making the Revolution* (Boston: Beacon Press, 1974), pp. 36–40.

2. Eileen Vogel, *Abortion and the Equal Rights Amendment: A Call to Common Sense* (Pittsburgh: People Concerned for the Unborn Child, 1978), pp. 2, 3.

3. *Ibid.*, p. 3.

4. *Christian Legal Defense and Educational Foundation Notebook,* Vol. 6, No. 3 (May 1980), p. 8.

5. "Don't Stoop to Equality," *The Constitutionalist* (July 1978), p. 8.

6. *The Library of Congress Congressional Record Research Bulletin,* No. HQ1428, U.S.D., p. S4375.

7. "Legality of Homosexual Marriage," *Yale Law Journal,* Vol. 82 (January 1973) pp. 573–589.

8. Vogel, p. 5.

Chapter 12: Conflicting Philosophies

1. Tim LaHaye, *The Battle for the Mind* (Old Tappan, N.J.: Fleming H. Revell Co., 1980), p. 27.

2. Tim LaHaye, *How We Got Our Bible* (Family Life Seminars, P.O. Box 1299, El Cajon, CA 92022).

3. LaHaye, *The Battle for the Mind,* pp. 78, 79.

4. *Humanist Manifestos I and II,* p. 8.

5. *Ibid.*, p. 18.
6. *Ibid.*, p. 19.
7. *Ibid.*, p. 16.
8. *Ibid.*
9. *Ibid.*
10. LaHaye, *The Battle for the Mind*, p. 83.
11. *Ibid.*, p. 55.
12. *Humanist Manifestos I and II*, p. 13.

Chapter 13: Feminine Influence on Our Nation

1. LaHaye, *The Battle for the Mind*, pp. 203, 204.